M000303785

Convergence with Nature

A Daoist Perspective

Convergence with Nature

A Daoist Perspective

David E. Cooper

green books

First published in 2012
by Green Books
Dartington Space, Dartington Hall,
Totnes TQ9 6EN

© David E. Cooper 2012

All rights reserved. No part of this book may be transmitted or
reproduced in any form or by any means without permission
in writing from the publisher.

Book design by Jayne Jones

Cover design by Rick Lawrence
rick@samskara-design.com

The photographs on pages 13, 81, 89, 117 and 138 are by the author.

Images on pages 72 and 106 (Freer Gallery of Art):
Page 72: Purchase, F1937.12 detail.
Page 106: Gift of Charles Lang Freer, F1915.36d.

Printed by T J International Ltd,
Padstow, Cornwall, UK

ISBN 978 0 85784 023 3

Contents

1   Orientation   8

2   Why Daoism?   17

3   Religion, technology, estrangement   26

4   Estrangement, environmentalism and 'otherness'   38

5   Nature in Daoism   45

6   On the Way (1): *dao*, world and unity   58

7   On the Way (2): *de*, virtues and sages   69

8   Mindfulness of nature   81

9   Nature, feeling and appreciation   94

10   Engaging with nature   107

11   Wilderness, wildness, wildlife   118

12   Intervening in nature   128

13   Intervening for nature?   141

Notes   153

Bibliography   160

Index   165

Acknowledgements

My thanks, first, to my friends and fellow philosophers, Graham Parkes and Simon P. James, for their detailed comments on draft chapters. No one writing a book in which environmental thought intersects with East Asian philosophy could wish for better-informed advisers. I greatly appreciate, too, the hard work done by the team at Green Books. I am especially grateful to John Elford for his advice on the form and style of the book, and to Alethea Doran for her impeccable copy-editing and her many helpful recommendations for improvements to the text.

References, abbreviations and transliteration

References within the text use the abbreviations indicated for the following works:

D   The *Daodejing*
Z   The Book of *Zhuangzi*
L   The Book of *Liezi*

References are to chapters of these works, e.g. (Z 2) refers to Chapter 2 of *The Book of Zhuangzi*.

References to other works are given in the notes, and details of all works cited are given in the bibliography.

Chinese terms and names are transliterated according to the modern Pinyin system. The older Wade-Giles transliterations of well-known terms and names are also given, in parentheses, when they first occur, e.g. 'Laozi (Lao Tzu)'.

Orientation

I set aside the book I was reading when, with the sun reddening, the evening fly-past of crows and green parrots began. For ten minutes, squadrons of birds sped above or through the grove of coconut palms that separated the Indian Ocean from the terrace of my room in a Sri Lankan guest house. The book, as it happened, was about wildlife, crows included. I rather associate Sri Lankan crows with reading books about nature. Once, a flock of them tore to pieces my copy of Gaston Bachelard's *The Poetics of Space*, left unguarded on a chair in a hotel garden. One chapter the birds shredded was called 'Nests'.

The author of the book I was reading until the crows and parrots returned to their roosts would approve of my putting it down. He would think it more important to watch the birds than to read about them. The choice between looking at birds and reading about them does not sound like a grave one. But a related decision worried me for some months. The book you are holding discusses how a person might live in an appropriate relationship to nature; to animals and natural places, both wild and, like farms and parks, 'humanised'. Now, what if *writing* about nature is the last form such a relationship should take? Maybe I should be engaging with the natural world in a more imme-diate, more muscular, and less parasitic way?

I haven't resolved this question, although some later remarks in this book bear on it. But I have learnt to ignore it. In this, I've been encouraged by reading authors who write good books about nature and, at the same time, seem to enjoy a good relationship to it.

Nature writing

Several of those books belong to the genre of 'nature writing', which has enjoyed a renaissance in recent years. Some fine contemporary authors[1] have written books that are worthy heirs to older classics such as Gilbert White's *The Natural History of Selborne*, Rousseau's *Reveries of a Solitary Walker*, Wordsworth's *A Guide through the District of the Lakes*, and Thoreau's *Walden*. Not all the authors I have in mind would usually be labelled 'nature writers', but their books also address questions about how human beings might properly relate to nature. Books, for example, on food – for questions about what and how we eat are, in part, about this relationship. Eating, as one of these writers puts it, is "our most profound engagement with the natural world".[2]

Nature writing is different from natural scientific writing, even when the authors are themselves botanists or zoologists and lace their books with scientific information and conjecture. For nature writers also, and essentially, convey their personal experience of wildlife and natural environments – their moods, emotions and fancies. As an early reviewer of White's *Selborne* observed, "not only is the understanding informed, but the imagination is touched".[3] To borrow from the title of a more recent book, the mountains that figure in nature writing are 'mountains of the mind'[4] as much as they are piles of limestone or granite.

Nature writing is different, too, from an environmentalist literature whose purpose is to enjoin us, with midnight said to be approaching, to 'save the planet'. It is not that all nature writers pass over environmental issues or eschew occasional calls to collective action. But the main orientation is a personal one. The concern is with an individual person's – the author's own – relationship with animals and natural places. The focus, therefore, is not the triply impersonal one of environmental ethicists and activists. That is, it is not on the formulation of general principles that are supposed to apply to everyone. Nor is it on devising policies for collective, mass action. Nor is it on actions and attitudes that, in keeping with our pragmatic age, are judged solely by the effects they have on life in general, on 'the human condition', on 'the environment', on the planet.

People whose orientation is a personal one – whose concern is with self-cultivation – get accused of egoism and moral indifference or nihilism. This is unfair. That the 'point of entry'[5] for ethical reflection is a concern for the good of the self does not mean that the 'point of exit' is without implications for the enlightened treatment of other people and living beings. The ancient philosophers of Greece, China and India, whose initial question was how an individual's life goes well, nearly all concluded that it does so only when the good of other people is attended to. If 'the virtues' refer to aspects of character that help a life to go well, then – so these ancients held – some of the virtues will be 'other-regarding'. Compassion, say, or respect. But it certainly doesn't follow that a relationship to the natural world that involves such other-regarding virtues has to be one of environmental activism or of commitment to universal principles of conduct that environmental ethicists seek to formulate. The relationship might be less strident, more intimate, less distracted by an ambition of effectiveness.

So, reflection on one's personal relationship to nature is not disjoined from ethical reflection. The contrast, rather, is with an entrenched, modern style of moral reason – a style that allows little scope for personal reflection, focused as it is on how 'one' should act or live. I act rightly, the modern story goes, when I do what it would be beneficial for everyone to do. For the ancients – and for me, and for many nature writers – this modern style of moral reason is lacking in realism, in attention to the world and human conduct as they actually are, instead of to what they might be if only . . .

Here's an illustration. I haven't eaten meat since 1979, when I was given Peter Singer's *Animal Liberation* as a Christmas present. It wasn't Singer's utilitarian arguments against the meat industry so much as his powerful descriptions of the conditions in factory farms that prevented me, on Boxing Day, from eating the cold turkey and ham. I still cannot eat meat and I am unmoved by the criticism that it would be disastrous if everyone were to give up eating meat. No lambs; no farmyards; no pastoral.

For a start, I have no idea – and nor do the critics – what a future world without meat-eaters would be like. Second, I know perfectly well that relatively few people will give up meat-eating. It would be frivolous to determine my relationship to animals – whether to eat them or not – on the basis of idle speculation about a world quite different from the one I am actually in. And perhaps worse than frivolous.

Maybe impersonal deliberation on how to relate to animals is in itself to be in a wrong relationship to them, one that prevents their figuring in our experience and emotional life as they should.

The question I address in this book – encouraged by the personal orientation of nature writing – is this:

What should my relationship to nature – to animals, to plants, to natural places – be like if it is to be an appropriate one and to contribute to the good of my life as a whole?

Each of you, of course, can address a similar question to yourself and then judge the relevance to it of the remarks I make on mine.

Some modern moods

My question is not asked out of the blue. It has a context. This context is provided by a number of *moods*, each of which – though ancient in provenance – is voiced in contemporary nature writing.

One mood is a sort of yearning – for what has variously been called convergence, harmony, intimacy, even identification or unity with nature on the part of human beings. This yearning is typically accompanied by a sense that a greater convergence or unity between people and nature once existed. So a second mood is one of nostalgia, of regret for the passing of an age when people were, it is said, less estranged from the natural world.

It is human beings themselves – or the civilisations they have developed – who are usually held responsible for this estrangement from nature. Hence, a third mood is one of disillusion, whether bitter or resigned, with humanity or at least with the course it has taken. There is a spectrum of moods within this. At one end is the bleak misanthropy of an author who identified more with peregrine falcons than with human beings, and who "longed . . . to let the human taint wash away in emptiness and silence", to lose his "predatory human shape" and to "shun" man, "that faceless horror of the stony places" with his "stink of death".[6] At the other, less dark, end of the spectrum bitterness is directed, not at humanity as such, but at a consumerist, hedonistic, hyper-technological society deemed responsible both for the devastation of the natural world and our estrangement from it.

One thing of which modern culture, with its predilections for technology, calculation and science, is often accused by nature writers is the loss of a sense of nature's mystery. This accusation implies an ambiguous attitude towards science, which is at once applauded for its discoveries about plants, animals and natural processes, but castigated for its pretension to be telling a complete story. Thoreau believed that we require natural phenomena to be "mysterious and unexplorable",[7] a point taken up by a later American writer who speaks of natural places as "mysteries" that cannot be "fathomed, biologically" and exhorts us, if we are to acquire any wisdom about nature, to "pay attention to mystery".[8] A fourth mood, then, is a feel for nature's mystery – for its ineffability – that cannot be dispelled by future scientific research.

I sympathise with these moods of yearning, nostalgia, bitterness or disillusion, and a feeling for mystery. Because I sympathise with them, my question about the shaping of an appropriate relationship to nature becomes more vital. For it is a question energised by the thought of a deep but atrophied convergence with the natural world that is worth reviving.

I want to justify these sympathies and to render attractive a certain conception of an appropriate relationship to the natural world. In doing so, there are different sources on which to draw. Poetry, for example, with its capacity, in an image or a line or two, to distil a mood. Disillusion with humanity's relationship to animals, for instance, which D. H. Lawrence famously recorded after throwing a log at a viper that was drinking at a trough:

... How paltry, how vulgar, what a mean act!
I despised myself and the voices of my accursed human education.[9]

Or there's the ability of a poet to give a fresh presence to an over-familiar place. Gain's Law is an austere, windswept hill in the Cheviots, close to my home. I hardly noticed it, until I read these spare verses, describing the place, by the Northumbrian poet Noel Hodgson:

Lumps of sheep
Scouring
Snow-plastered heather.

Their horned heads
Black-splotching
The Whitescape.

Straggled
Whin bushes
Writhing at stabs
Of icy wind.[10]

I now walk over Gain's Law on snowy mornings with a new attention and a fellow-feeling for the sheep and the bushes.

Direct, sinewy engagement with natural places – when kayaking, backpacking or climbing – is another source on which to draw, as are the gentler reveries of the solitary walker or watcher. Simple, close observation of little things – of wild flowers, insects, pebbles – can also evoke and invite a mood of yearning or nostalgia. As may thoughtful reflection on the place of plants, animals, lakes and hills in human culture and the civilised imagination.

Below Gain's Law.

Philosophy's roles

As this last remark implies, one source will be philosophy, my own métier. Philosophy, though, is not a single source, but a range of traditions, practices and speculations. Several of these bear upon the concerns of this book – upon, especially, the idea of human convergence with nature.

To begin with, this is an idea that needs support from general accounts, of the type that philosophy endeavours to provide, of human beings and their world. For, if certain accounts are correct, then convergence sounds to be unattractive or impossible. Take, for instance, the view that is forcibly expressed in Matthew Arnold's ironically titled poem 'In harmony with nature':

> Know, man hath all which Nature hath, but more,
> And in that more lies all his hopes of good. [...]
> Man must begin, know this, where Nature ends;
> Nature and man can never be fast friends.[11]

If the worth of human beings consists in cultural achievements made possible only through battling the processes of nature, then convergence with nature is a step back towards savagery.

Or take the view, popular among many scientists, that the world of experience – of birdsong, tree resin, flowers – is illusion, a veil between us and the real world of invisible particles of which only physicists have an understanding. Who wants to seek for intimacy or unity with what is, in effect, a phantom? A yearning for convergence requires, therefore, different philosophies of human beings and the world from the views just mentioned.

The idea of convergence, moreover, will remain a coarse one without analysis, of this and of related ideas (unity, identity, intimacy). This needs to be an analysis, of the kind philosophers try to provide, that exposes the implications of the idea for practice and perception. Certainly, there are plenty of questions about these implications that can be raised. Here are a few:

Is gardening a model of convergence – of a 'fusion' between culture and nature – or is it instead an exercise in human dominion over nature?

Is enjoyment of the beauty of animals, trees and lakes an authentic form of intimacy with nature, or is it symptomatic of an 'anthropocentric' stance towards nature as a resource for sensual titillation?

What of the fear people reasonably have of dangerous places and animals, and their recognition that nature is in part a theatre of cruelty and horror? "It's rough out there and chancy", observes an American nature writer, "gruesome ... grotesque ... a universal chomp".[12] Is this a reason for estrangement, for resisting any identification with nature? Or are fear and horror, as they seem to be for her, ingredients in an honest communion with nature?

With questions like these multiplying, pious talk of convergence or oneness with nature must give way to disciplined reflection on its meaning. Such talk will also remain glib in the absence of perspicuous descriptions of living things and natural phenomena as these figure in experience. Consider our experience of animals. "Our self-perception", remarks a primatologist, "is never animal-free".[13] People's view of people is partly shaped by a perception of their similarities to and contrasts with dogs, apes and other creatures. This perception needs to be made salient if the significance of animals in our lives is to be understood. Perspicuous description that exposes the significance of experiences in the larger structures of human practice and understanding – in our 'forms of life' – is the ambition of the philosophical approach known as phenomenology.[14] Here, then, is another philosophical source on which to draw.

Finally, an older conception of philosophy should be recalled. For the ancient thinkers of Greece and Asia, philosophy was less a body of knowledge than a practice of self-cultivation or self-transformation, of right attunement to the world. Philosophy, for them, was orientated in the first instance to the Good, not to the True, even if attainment of the Good turns out to require respect for the True.

This ancient conception contains an important lesson. The proper response to questions about life – including ones about an appropriate relationship to nature – is not a narrowly cognitive one, not a matter of mouthing a correct answer. For in order for answers to penetrate – to be 'deeply cultivated', as Buddhists say – and thereby to shape one's life, the mind must already be appropriately attuned or transformed. 'Life', we hear, 'should be lived in harmony with nature'. Certainly – but if the words are not to remain glib, pious and formulaic, they must be heard by someone suitably attuned; emotionally and physically prepared for the words to penetrate. Philosophy, on the ancient conception, is a precondition for hearing.

It is often said that, for the ancients, philosophy was 'a way of life',[15] not a corpus of theory and argument. That is right, provided that 'a way of life' is used with due weight, and not lightly (as when it is said, for example, that 'clubbing' has become a way of life among today's youth). A way – a path, for instance – typically goes somewhere; it has a destination; it leads or guides those who are on it. Staying on it may require self-discipline, balance, fitness and intelligence. The metaphor of a way is a rich one, nowhere more so than in the Chinese philosophical tradition whose very name employs the metaphor: Daoism, the philosophy of the *dao* (*tao*, the Way). Daoism, I want to show, has resources and an angle of vision suited to addressing the question about an appropriate relationship to nature.

On the evening following the one by the Indian Ocean that I described earlier, the crows and parrots again begin their fly-past silhouetted against a reddening sun. But this time, I can't concentrate. Behind me, in the restaurant, sits and shouts a group of lobster-pink tourists who have been combining beer and arrack for six hours. They are oblivious to the sea, the palms, the falling sun and the chattering squadrons of birds. Theirs, I feel, is not – on this evening's evidence, at least – an appropriate relationship to the natural world. I want to explore how a Daoist perspective helps to secure this impression.

Why Daoism?

There is a style of Chinese landscape painting that is especially associated with Daoism. I am now looking at a painting in this style in the book that is open on my desk. It is a well-known copy of a lost picture by Fan Kuan (fl. 990–1030), called 'Travellers Among Mountains and Streams'. In the foreground are some diminutive figures, the travellers, dwarfed by wooded crags and a huge bare mountain. I turn to a new page where there is a photograph of another painting in the genre, 'Listening Quietly to Soughing Pines', by Ma Lin (thirteenth century). Here, a small figure sits by some gnarled trees, beyond which mountains rise above a misty valley.*

Nature and people in Chinese art

Western commentary on such paintings usually takes their message to be the puniness and insignificance of human beings compared with the vastness and might of nature. But this is not a convincing interpretation. True, the fishermen, farmers, hermits or travellers depicted are small in size relative to the landscape, but they are not figures cowed or bowed in awestruck wonder or terror. As the author of an early essay on landscape painting, Zong Bing (third–fourth century BCE), explains, it is relaxed delight, "gratification of the spirit", and reflective imagination that are induced by the places he paints.[1] Moreover, the landscapes are typically not untouched wildernesses but environments that are, to a degree, humanised, by the presence of little temples, boats or huts.

* Pictured on pages 19 and 21.

It would in any case be unfaithful to the Daoist understanding of human beings' relationship to nature to construe this art as representing their total cosmic insignificance. It is true that, in the texts, there is an emphasis on human beings' dependence on the natural order, and a refusal to elevate human worth over that of other living beings. There is even the occasional passage that speaks of a human being as "no more than a mere pebble or a bush on a great mountain" (Z 17). But, as this same text (the *Zhuangzi*) explains, human beings have a special role in "nourishing" things and "bringing the world into harmony" (Z 33). Moreover, the very distinction between what is owed to 'heaven' (nature, in this context) and to humanity is not sharp. The sage recognises that "neither the heavenly nor the human . . . win[s] out over the other" (Z 6).

We might see the little men in Chinese landscape paintings not as symbols of puny impotence but as people reflectively engaged with the natural environments that surround them. This reflection need not be heavy-duty, furrow-browed cogitation. It may instead be gentle reverie; an intelligent and supple alertness to, say, the sound of a pine tree, more than a process of deliberation. It may be the kind of reflection Zong Bing enjoyed when, while viewing cliffs and peaks and groves, he let people and things "live in my imagination and . . . come together in my spirit and in my thoughts".

This would connect the paintings with a poetry that is also associated with Daoism. In poems of the Tang dynasty and earlier, a recurrent theme is the official who has lived and worked in the city but now escapes into the countryside, there to meditate, reflect and purify himself. A master of this style is Tao Qian (or Tao Yuan-ming, 365–427), for ten years a minor official but without "desire for glory or profit", who returns to his smallholding to rediscover peace. Leaving "far behind thoughts of the world", he may "find again the meaning of life". No longer a prisoner in the "dust-filled trap" of the city, and getting "back to nature", he is "waking up". In his simple hut, in chrysanthemums, in the mountain air and in the song of birds, he discerns "a great truth" that he will try, but perhaps fail, to express in his verse.[2]

Tao Qian is usually described as a Daoist, and he was clearly receptive to Daoist thoughts and moods. And this is how I see the little men in the landscape paintings – less as card-carrying Daoist adepts

'Travellers Among Mountains and Streams', Fan K'uan.
© National Palace Museum, Taiwan, Republic of China

than as people who, perhaps through meeting with travelling sages, engage in reflections on nature that are adjacent to those articulated in the classic Daoist texts. Their reflections are, one might say, in a Daoist key – and so are the thoughts expressed in this book.

In a Daoist key

But why 'thoughts in a Daoist key', and not simply 'Daoist thoughts'? By allowing that my remarks may modulate rather than strictly render Daoist themes, I avoid entanglement in issues which, in a short book, I need to skirt. For a start, I avoid scholarly disputes over the exact meaning of this or that claim made in Daoist texts. The two main works on which I draw, the *Daodejing* (*Tao Te Ching*) and The Book of *Zhuangzi* (Chuang Tzu), which were finally compiled in the third century BCE, are both difficult to interpret. The 81 verses of the former are too terse to dictate a single interpretation, while Zhuangzi's use of anecdotes, irony and other rhetorical devices in place of 'straight' discourse opens the meaning of many of his utterances to dispute. Nor is either text entirely consistent – the result of each being the product, over many years, of more than one hand. For instance, Zhuangzi probably composed only the first seven or 'inner' chapters of the book that bears his name. Informed commentators can disagree on whether, say, the *Daodejing* is Machiavellian in its politics, or whether Zhuangzi is a sceptic. My construals of the texts – especially in Chapters 6 and 7 on the central notions of *dao* and *de* – are, I hope, plausible. But I don't intend to embark on a scholarly defence of them.

Next, I avoid entanglement in certain demarcation issues. One of these concerns the relationship of Daoism to Confucianism, which commentators used to pit against one another. The latter, it was said, attracted "those who wear official buttons and those who kowtow to them". For Daoists, Confucianism was "too decorous, too reasonable" and they preferred to "go about with dishevelled hair and bare feet".[3] Among contemporary scholars, a more nuanced perception prevails, and they remind us that the authors of the classic texts, between the fifth and third centuries BCE, did not classify themselves as Confucians, Daoists or -ists of any kind. The division into schools of philosophy was the invention of later historians.

'Listening Quietly to Soughing Pines', Ma Lin.
© National Palace Museum, Taiwan, Republic of China

On our topic of a human being's relationship to nature, it is stressed these days that, for Confucians as well as for Daoists, this is an important dimension of the life of 'the consummate person'. In a passage of the *Analects*[4] popular among modern Chinese readers, Confucius asks his companions about their ambitions. Three of them answer that theirs is to serve in some official capacity in public life, but the fourth, Zengxi, replies that he would prefer, in the company of a few young people, to bathe in the river and 'revel in the cool breezes'. Confucius "heaved a great sigh, and said, 'I'm with Zengxi'".

It may be, then, that some thoughts in a Daoist key are also in a Confucian key and even have their origins in a Confucian text. This is a matter that I leave to experts – as I do the relationship between Daoism and the Chan (or, in Japanese, Zen) school of Buddhism, which developed in China between the sixth and eight centuries. Close affinities between the two were soon recognised – unsurprisingly, given that Chan's development owed as much to Daoist influence as to Indian Buddhist doctrine. The attention Chan pays to relationships with natural environments – something manifest in the Buddhist gardens of East Asia – is one significant area of affinity with Daoism. If some thoughts expressed in this book have a Buddhist provenance, so be it; they may still be in a Daoist key.

A final demarcation issue is internal to Daoism. Sixty years ago, the foremost Chinese historian of ideas urged that Daoist philosophy be "kept carefully distinguished from the Daoist religion".[5] And for a long time commentators did just that, sharply distinguishing the 'early' or 'philosophical' Daoism of the classic texts from the 'religious' or, pejoratively, 'superstitious' and 'magical' Daoism that emerged during the second and third centuries CE. The latter was to become China's main indigenous religion, replete with priests, temples, rituals and the deification of Laozi (Lao Tzu), the supposed author of the *Daodejing*.

As with the distinction between Daoism and Confucianism, perception of the contrast between 'the two Daoisms' is now more nuanced. If religious Daoism is dedication to 'biospiritual' cultivation of the self[6] and an effort to establish communion between human beings, the earth and heavenly spirits, then – so it is argued – the seeds were there in the earlier, 'philosophical' texts. My Daoist perspective is mainly drawn from these earlier texts, but I don't take sides over the continuity or otherwise between 'the two Daoisms'. Nor, in fact, do I ignore the literature of 'religious' Daoism, for this contains some interesting pronouncements on people's relationship to nature.

Daoist moods

The question remains why it is to a Daoist perspective that I turn as a resource for enquiry into a person's appropriate relationship to the natural world.

Early this clear and icy morning, I took a long walk in a valley on the edge of the Cheviot mountains, not far from Gain's Law, the subject of a poem I cited in Chapter 1. Perhaps because that chapter, written a few days before, was fresh in my mind, I found myself rehearsing the moods it discussed – yearning, nostalgia, disillusion, a sense of mystery.

As I walked, it also struck me that an artist perched to my left and painting the landscape through which I was moving would depict a scene not unlike those in the works by Ma Lin or Fan Kuan. Pine-topped hillsides steeply descend to a stream which runs through a valley, and alongside the stream a diminutive human figure is walking.

Having imagined myself into the landscapes depicted by Chinese artists, it seemed natural to associate myself with the little men who appear in them, and to speculate that – as they walk, fish or listen to the sound of pine trees – they also experience the moods just mentioned. Not just natural, but compelling: for these are moods attested to in Daoist texts, and conveyed in the paintings and poems of artists under the sway of these texts.

And here is the first and simplest reason for turning to a Daoist perspective. It, too, registers the moods with which I earlier stated sympathy. Daoist texts articulate a yearning for convergence with nature, nostalgia for a lost intimacy with the natural world, disillusion with humanity or its products, and a feeling for the mystery of nature. How these moods are articulated, elaborated and justified will emerge later – but it would be useful, at this point, to cite some indicative remarks from the *Daodejing*.

A recurring proposal in that work is that human beings should learn from and emulate natural processes if their lives are to go well. In this respect (among others), people should seek to commune and converge with nature. "The supreme good is like water" (D 8). Not only does it benefit living things, but it does so through flowing in a gentle, supple, non-contentious way that is a model for effective human behaviour. More generally, people should "follow the way of earth". This is because:

Earth follows the way of heaven.
Heaven follows the way of the *dao*.
And the *dao* follows the way of spontaneity. (D 25)

By modelling themselves on nature, therefore, people share in the spontaneity, the naturalness, of the Way itself.

The book looks back, with some nostalgia, to a time when this convergence was greater than it has since become: to an age when the human population was smaller, technology more simple, travel less of an imperative, desires more modest, and men did not take up arms against one another. Hardly leaving their own villages, people's lives were contented. A return to this age would mean that people could once again "relish their food, feel comfortable in their homes and delight in their customs" (D 80). As the mention of technology and arms suggests, people's estrangement from the natural world is blamed, not on fate, divine punishment or human nature as such, but on economic, political and cultural developments. An obsession with profit, with the satisfaction of desires, with the acquisition of knowledge, and with rules and rituals has put an end to the "plainness and simplicity" of an earlier, less anxious age (D 19). Warfare at once reflects and intensifies this process, destroying the "peace and quiet" that were once people's "highest ideals" (D 31).

The *Daodejing* begins, famously, with the remark that "the *dao* that can be named is not the constant *dao*". A few lines later, this nameless mystery is held to be "the origin of heaven and earth" (of nature or the universe, in effect). A deep enigma or mystery, too, is the connection or "unity" between the *dao* and "the myriad things" for whose existence it is ultimately responsible (D1). The Daoist sage, therefore, experiences the natural world as doubly mysterious – in its origin and in its relationship to this origin. This is one reason for the tart remarks, in later chapters, on chattering scholars and would-be sages. "Those who talk about [the *dao*] do not know" (D 56), and we should strive to "get rid of the learning" which gives rise to such chatter (D 19).

There is a further sympathy of mine which is shared by Daoist texts: this time for a style of ethical reflection.

The story is told of a gnarled, dishevelled old fisherman who encounters a travelling teacher and his companions as they rest on their journey. He learns from the companions that the teacher is a benevolent, conscientious man, committed to codifying rites and rules of conduct, to political reform and to benefiting the world. The teacher, seeing the fisherman smile at their words, asks him to explain this wry response. What he then gets in reply is advice – gentle, polite, but firm – to change his ways. Instead of occupying himself with the conduct of others, the teacher should, in the first instance, "earnestly cultivate [his] own person . . . the genuine in [him]". Whereas rites and rules are merely "the customs of the times", the genuine or authentic is "the means by which we draw on heaven" and is "spontaneous". At the end of the fisherman's lecture, the teacher acknowledges that he has been listening to a man who "possesses the Way".

This story is told in the *Zhuangzi* (Z 31), and the teacher is none other than Confucius, deferring – as he does elsewhere in the book – to the superior wisdom of a Daoist sage. One such sage from an earlier chapter puts the fisherman's point more bluntly. Those who attend to what "suits other people" before "what is suitable to themselves" – who act on "elevated principles of goodwill and duty", of benevolence and righteousness – are liable to commit "debased" and "aberrant" deeds (Z 8).

Earlier, I endorsed those ancient traditions in which the 'point of entry' for moral reflection is not general principles of actions or their outcomes, but self-cultivation. Daoism is one such tradition. The Daoist focus is not on benevolence or duty, but on 'fineness' in the 'power' or 'virtue' (*de,* or *te*) of the self-cultivated person (Z 8).

In asking about an appropriate relationship to nature, the Daoist too is asking a personal question, concerning a relationship to the natural world that enables an individual's life to go well, to be 'fine'. In its style of enquiry and in its moods, then, Daoism promises to be a source on which to draw. A Daoist key is one to be attuned to.

Religion, technology, estrangement

It would be nice to present a Daoist vision of an appropriate relationship to nature without delay. But, first, there are some sceptical voices to be listened to. In responding to them, however, important components of this vision begin to emerge.

According to one voice – a chorus, more likely – estrangement from the natural world, though its origins may lie in a Middle Eastern religion, is an essentially Western phenomenon. Re-convergence with nature is, correspondingly, a Western project. Estrangement is the result of developments in theology, science and technology with which ancient Chinese thinkers had no acquaintance. Nothing they had to say could therefore have much relevance to the ambition of re-convergence. Unfamiliar with the disease, they could not contribute to its diagnosis or cure.

On this view, popular in pronouncements on 'our ecological crisis', estrangement is the joint toxic product of theology and technology.

Theology and 'the ecological crisis'[1]

The contribution of the Abrahamic religions to Western thought, one hears, has been to teach that the human mind or soul is a distinct 'substance' from any physical entity, and that the good of human beings is the purpose of God's creation. Strictly, one need not be a religious believer to accept a dualist account of mind and body and an anthropocentric notion of the universe's purpose. Historically, however, these have had their main home and rationale in monotheistic religion.

Mind–body dualism, it is charged, sets human beings apart from or 'over against' everything else, thereby compromising their affinity with nature. So does the anthropocentric teaching, since it regards nature as an instrumental means to human well-being. As for the present fate of natural environments, so the claim continues, theology might not have mattered were it not for the development of modern technology, which has enabled people to practise what religion preached. With its help, they have now turned the world into a resource over which humanity, now truly elevated above nature, exercises sovereign control.

Such is the familiar narrative of modern humanity's religiously rooted estrangement from nature. However, it is an unpersuasive one. To begin with, it is only within a much larger context of related beliefs that the dualist doctrine of mind and body as two distinct stuffs could encourage a sense of estrangement. It's not hard to think of other religious beliefs that would, as it were, neutralise this effect: the conviction, for example, that mental and physical processes unfold in divinely tuned harmony with one another. To engender a sense of estrangement, dualism requires the further belief – a tenet of modern science rather than of theology – that the mind is relatively insulated from the physical world, since it can directly affect nothing except the body in which it is lodged. It was not Descartes' dualism so much as his rejection of an older picture of the mind's powers over the outside world that earns him a place in the narrative of estrangement. This picture, still visible in the Renaissance, was that the mind, in an 'occult' way, directly brings about events in the world. Descartes endorsed Galileo's conception of the physical world as an enclosed mechanism, one that made no room for malicious intentions, the sincerity of prayer, or any other mental state directly to produce worldly effects. It is a conception that excludes a sense of interdependence between mind and world.

A similar point applies to the anthropocentric view of creation. Only in the context of further beliefs could this incline people towards a sense of estrangement from nature. It would not do this, for instance, if it was believed – as by some contemporary theologians – that the human good at which creation aims consists precisely in compassionate stewardship over nature.

The religious doctrines in question, then, are not sufficient to inspire a sense of estrangement. Nor are they are necessary for such a sense, for there are many positions in which theology plays no part, but which exhort us to regard nature as alien to us. One was articulated in the Matthew Arnold poem quoted on page 14. "Man must begin . . . where Nature ends" expresses the creed of T. H. Huxley,[2] the Darwinian for whom everything that makes people truly human – law, morality, education – is a 'combat' against nature, against the blind 'cosmic process' of natural selection. Huxley was no dualist and no advocate of a cosmic purpose. For him, there is no metaphysical gulf between human and other beings, but there is an 'enmity' between nature and the cultural achievements that rescue us from animal existence. Views such as Huxley's have done more than theology to promote in some people a sense of separation from nature.

But maybe neither the theological doctrines, nor those which rival them, should be given much weight in an explanation of our sense of estrangement. They look too intellectual, too remote from everyday intercourse and experience with the natural world, to play a significant role in shaping these.

This morning was again clear and cold, a morning for a walk in the 'icy-boned mountains', as the poet Noel Hodgson calls them, that I see from my study window. The walk is around a pond, along a path fringed by pines and sycamores. To some of these trees, local people have attached bird boxes. On top of one box, a red squirrel sits stock-still, checking me out. Through the sunlit trees, finches and tits fly to and from their chosen boxes, and on the pond two ducks are waddling in search of a break in the ice. I could sense the squirrel's apprehension, feel the birds' pleasure at the sunshine, and share in the ducks' relief when they plopped into a hole where the ice had thawed.

These were small, modest experiences of convergence. The ability or otherwise to enjoy such experiences surely doesn't depend on acceptance or rejection of a couple of theological doctrines. If convergence of the kind such experiences illustrate has become rarer and more difficult, the explanation lies elsewhere.

But why, in that case, is the theologically charged narrative of estrangement so popular? Perhaps it is self-serving. People who tell this narrative typically reject the religious premises: *they* are too scientifically savvy, too up-to-date, to endorse the myths of dualism and creation's purpose. So it is not *they* who bear responsibility for estrangement, but those insufficiently enlightened people who succumbed to those myths. It is comfortable – and comforting – to blame things on doctrines to which only other people give credence.

A philosopher's hut

No one could say that modern technology is too remote from everyday experience to help shape it. Each time I switch on a car engine, computer, coffee-maker or DVD player, I connect into experiences enabled and constrained by technology.

But does modern technology foster estrangement from the natural world in which it intrudes? Not according to some of its enthusiasts – the Italian 'Futurist' F. T. Marinetti, for example, who in 1908 invited his readers to "hymn the man at the steering-wheel whose ideal axis passes through the centre of the earth"[3] uniting him with it more emphatically than through making cheese or spinning wool. Nor according to eighteenth-century garden makers whose employment of the latest earth-shifting or hydraulic technology was not, in their eyes, a conquest of alien nature but a means, as Horace Walpole put it, to restore to nature its 'honours'.[4]

These examples indicate that it is not the use of technological hardware – motor cars, diggers, pumps – which by itself promotes a sense of estrangement from the natural world. This will be the product, rather, of a spirit and comportment with which technology may be allied. This is a point, we will see, appreciated by Daoist thinkers. But before returning to China, a detour via the Black Forest.

In 1922, the German philosopher Martin Heidegger, then in his early thirties, had built for him a small chalet, or 'hut', on the edge of a village high in the mountains of the Schwarzwald. Over the next 50 years, most of his writing was done here. It was not simply that the place 'up there' afforded peace and quiet in which to work. More importantly, as Heidegger explained in a radio broadcast, this work was "sustained and guided" by the landscape, where he "experienced the great comings and goings of the seasons", and where mountains, trees and lakes "penetrated daily existence":

> As soon as I go back up there . . . I am simply transported into
> [my] work's own rhythm . . . People in the city often wonder
> whether one gets lonely up in the mountains . . . But it isn't
> loneliness, it is solitude . . . Solitude has the peculiar and origi-
> nal power of . . . projecting our whole existence into the vast
> nearness of the presence of things.[5]

Especially sustained and guided were Heidegger's meditations on the
'homelessness' of people in the modern world. His focus, here, was not
the domestic dislocation caused by great wars and industrial migra-
tions. Instead it was on a sense of estrangement from the earth and
from the natural places where human beings once lived as communities. Today, he rhetorically asks, what are animals and plants to us except
objects for "use, embellishment and entertainment"?

Heidegger's term for the cause of homelessness is 'technology'.
This names, however, not machinery and industrial processes, but a
distinctive and increasingly dominant style of experiencing or 'revealing' the world. Technology reveals nature as 'equipment' for human
beings to use, a 'reserve' to draw on, a resource. A river, say, is revealed

Heidegger's hut in the Schwarzwald. © Digne Meller-Marcovicz

as a source for generating electricity, or a place to supply coachloads of tourists with pleasures or thrills.

Technology is inseparable from tendencies that feed and reinforce its way of revealing the world. From the prestige of science, for example, whose grey, mathematical picture of nature obscures the vision of what "stirs and strives ... assails us and enthrals us as landscape". Inseparable, too, from what Heidegger calls 'humanism' – a hubristic conception of 'man as the measure of all things', the autonomous arbiter of value and truth, answerable only to standards that humanly constructed systems of morality and enquiry have determined. Inseparable, therefore, from a related inflation of the worth, dignity and rights of human beings as creatures uniquely able to determine their own lives. And inseparable, finally, from a 'boredom' which creates not only a need for distracting entertainment but also a need for a relentlessly busy pursuit of goals and targets. In this febrile atmosphere, people do things not so much in order to satisfy desires as for the sake of having something to chase after.[6]

This may sound like bleak sociological analysis, a symptom of a war-ravaged, destitute age, but for Heidegger, 'homelessness' is not simply a social problem. It represents "the forgetfulness of Being" – a loss of the sense of a mysterious source of things. This was the sense which once sustained men and women in their confidence that their lives had something to answer to and be measured by.

In one essay, Heidegger uses the term '*dao*' for this mysterious source, the "great hidden stream which moves all things along and makes [a] way for everything".[7] This reflects his fascination with Daoism. He admired those Chinese paintings in which little men are dwarfed by surrounding mountains, and he liked to have photos of himself taken, seated in front of his chalet with the hills rising behind it, that evoke these paintings. Heidegger's son relates that a well in the garden had special significance for his father: a metaphor for the mysterious 'hidden stream' that was itself a metaphor for the Way. In 1946, Heidegger worked, with a native speaker of Chinese, on a translation – never completed and now lost – of the *Daodejing*.

Heidegger's insights into estrangement are indebted to Daoism, and in turn are helpful for our understanding of the Daoist attitude to nature.[8]

Daoism, technology and estrangement

According to the popular view discussed earlier in this chapter, ancient peoples had no experience of the factors responsible for estrangement from the natural world. It is an essentially modern, Western phenomenon.

But Daoist philosophers were familiar with ideas and developments comparable to those highlighted in the popular view. With, for a start, the idea – albeit one they rejected – that mind and body are distinct substances. The 'mind–heart' (xin) was thought of as a bodily organ, and while Chinese cosmology allowed for nature spirits and the souls of ancestors, these did not belong to another, non-physical realm. Like everything else, including human minds and bodies, they were constituted by qi, the energy that enables all life and motion. Because it had never been entrenched in Chinese cosmology, a dualist doctrine was not credited with responsibility for estrangement.

Daoist thinkers were acquainted, too, with the belief that the world was designed by a divine power for the good of human beings. Belief in something like a supreme god, Shang Di (Lord of the Shang People), had atrophied, however, long before the compilation of the Daoist texts. Shang Di had given way to impersonal powers, 'heaven' (tian) and the dao.

These philosophers were also familiar with an anthropocentric understanding of the world's purpose. While this was not held responsible for a sense of alienation from nature, it was deemed worthy of refutation. In the Liezi (L 8), a sparky young boy takes a visiting dignitary to task for praising heaven's generosity in providing grain, birds and fish for people to eat. "It is not as your lordship says", complains the boy, "the myriad things between heaven and earth, born in the same way that we are, do not differ from us in kind". Our species, he continues, is "no nobler than another" and different species are "not bred for each other's sake". There is no more reason to think that heaven bred animals "for the sake of man" than to suppose that it "bred man for the sake of the mosquitoes and gnats" which feed on human beings. No creatures exist in order to serve other creatures: it's simply that some – the 'stronger' – are able to dominate and exploit others.

The classics of Chinese philosophy – Confucian, Daoist and others – were written or compiled during the 'Warring States' period (c.480–221 BCE). Despite the turmoil suggested by that name, China became, and for millennia remained, the world's largest and wealthiest agrarian economy. This was due in part to technological advances – in wheat production, iron making, tool manufacture, road and canal building, and irrigation. Within a few years of the deaths of Zhuangzi and Mencius (Mengzi), the governor of Shu state embarked on the greatest public works project yet undertaken anywhere – diverting a river, contouring hills, creating a waterway – to convert Sichuan into the rice bowl of the empire.

So Daoist thinkers were not unfamiliar with intrusive technological development. Their concern, however, was not the new technology as such, but with an approach to life that preoccupation with technical progress encourages. This concern is voiced by a peasant who rejects the offer of a new-fangled, labour-saving "contrivance which in one day would irrigate a hundred fields". The peasant "made an angry face and said with a sneer" that "'whoever has contrivances with tricks to make them go is sure to have activities with tricks to make them go'". Such profit-making contrivances, in effect, corrupt the "mind–heart" (*xin*), since they are used by people who themselves lead contrived or "tricky" lives, and lose contact with "the pure and simple … and vital". They are people whom "the Way will not sustain" (Z 12).

For Daoists, as for Heidegger, it is not technology as hardware or engineering, but as a way of experiencing the world, which estranges from nature, from the Way itself. And for Daoists, as for their German admirer, this way of experiencing the world colludes with further tendencies of estrangement.

To begin with, impressive technological modifications of nature – changing a river's course, say – reinforce a hubristic confidence in human capacities, autonomy and worth. This obscures something appreciated by the sages of old, that human achievements are dependent on what is not of human making. This is the point of passages where Daoist writers accuse their contemporaries of attributing to human effort alone what crucially involves the work of heaven. The "men of old" recognised "what is heaven's" and "did not let man intrude on heaven" (Z 6), for they understood, as Guo Xiang, an early commentator on the *Zhuangzi*, put it,[9] that a human body "requires all of heaven and earth to support it" and that "human doing has its own limited range".

There are two important realms of human concern – for living well and for understanding or wisdom – where excessive self-esteem is particularly pernicious. In the *Daodejing*, the story is told of a decline: from submission to the Way to submission to principles of benevolence and righteousness and, eventually, to the rites that so prominently dictated Chinese behaviour (D 38). The story, in effect, is one of increasing confidence that human beings can and should live according to rules and conventions of their own making.

Equally hubristic is "lust after knowledge" of a calculating, pragmatic kind subject to economic and technological imperatives. This lust arises in "disordered" times and, in turn, serves to increase disorder. It is the kind of knowledge or "cleverness" exemplified in ingenious methods for the excessive trapping of birds, fish and animals, thereby causing disorder in the sky, lakes and woods (Z 10). It's the kind of knowledge, too, behind those "tricky" irrigation devices rejected by the angry old peasant.

Both these tendencies – erecting systems of values and rules; pursuing clever technical know-how – mark an abdication from guidance by the *dao*, a source beyond human contrivance that gives measure to the ways of human beings. Both tendencies are lamented in the *Daodejing*. Knowledge "lusted" after is a "detriment" to society, whereas true understanding of a "standard" for life is "profound (or enigmatic) virtue" (*xuande*) that "returns to", and "naturally complies with", "the origin of all things" (D 65).

Technology, lust for knowledge, and an obsession with rules are connected. They belong within a larger economy of mutually reinforcing tendencies and attitudes. The rites, rules, taboos, laws and edicts that people are constantly creating; the weapons and other technical contrivances they invent; the clever skills and techniques they learn – all this is indicative of a restless, hyperactive society where tranquillity and contentment have been lost (D 57).

This is a society where "the multitude [must] all have something to do" (D 20), where people are "scurrying around even when sitting still" in pursuit of some goal (Z 4). Things were different in earlier times:

The genuine human beings of old . . . did not aspire to com-
pleteness, did not plan their affairs in advance. In this way, they
could be wrong or they could be right, but without regret
and without self-satisfaction. (Z 6)

The busy planning and pursuit of goals at once responds to and generates desires, including those that are complicit in warfare and grand
hydrology projects. When desire dominates, horses are used in battle
instead of farming, and "the worst calamity" that can afflict people is
"the desire to acquire" (D 4). Criticism of "profit-seeking" and acquisitive desire as destructive of peace of mind is a main theme in a short
work, the *Neiye* ('Inner life' or 'Cultivation'). One complaint is that
desire distorts the understanding, so that people and things are viewed,
not in "their proper perspective", but only in terms of the satisfaction
they yield. The theme is continued by Zhuangzi, who regrets a "characteristic inclination" of people in his century – the invidious judgement of things as right or wrong, true or false, in accordance with
one's "likes and dislikes" (Z 5).

Most of the desires that incline action and judgement in these
times of discontent are not inborn fixtures of human psychology. The
"pleasure, anger, worry, anxiety" which, as the *Neiye* explains, activate
or result from desires are symptoms of a general restlessness and
"mental agitation" that gives to the times their distinctive stamp. Lacking peace of mind, fearful of boredom, people are pushed and pulled
this way and that. It's as if they develop desires in order to then have
something to do and aim at.

Unlike the story of estrangement that concentrates on religious
doctrines which are rejected by the narrators, there is nothing comfortable in the Daoist account. For among the tendencies held to be
complicit in estrangement are ones that, today, are applauded. It has
become a good thing, it seems, to have passionate convictions and
challenging ambitions, to be always active and on the move, to enjoy
life's pleasures to the full, to accumulate evermore knowledge and
information, to become proud of the construction of gigantic stadi-
ums or tunnels, to exercise ever greater 'choice' among goods and
goals and companions, to attribute absolute worth and dignity to the
human person, to create one's own 'table of values' and to scoff at the

old delusion that these tables, these moralities, are anything but the 'life choices' made by human beings.

There is nothing comforting in the thought that re-convergence with the natural world requires resistance to much of what is honoured in our times.

'Letting-be'

War-torn Germany in the twentieth century was a different place from China of the Warring States era. Both places, however, were perceived by some of their thinkers as sites of alienation from the natural world – and for comparable reasons. An affinity between Heidegger's reflections – on hubris, 'humanism', technology, restless boredom and much else – and thoughts expressed in ancient Daoist texts is unmistakable. One sees why Heidegger liked to appear in photos that evoke Chinese paintings of sages sitting or walking in vast, mountainous landscapes.

Here is a further affinity. Heidegger gives the name '*Gelassenheit*' ('releasement', 'letting-be') to an authentic experience of the world starkly opposed to the technological 'way of revealing'. Zhuangzi articulated a similar contrast two millennia earlier, when he opposed the inclination to experience things in the light of one's prejudices to a steady willingness to "follow along with the way each thing (spontaneously) is of itself, going by whatever *it* affirms as right, without trying to add anything to the process of life" (Z 5). This remark invokes the famous Daoist antithesis to the restless, agitated, opinionated pursuit of goals, technical knowledge, profit, and pleasure: *wu wei*. Literally, this means 'non-action' or 'not doing', but since the sage who 'conducts his affairs through non-action' (D 2) is not a supine couch-potato or in trance-like immobility, *wu wei* is often rendered less literally – as, say, unintrusive or unforceful action.

More suggestive are characterisations of *wu wei* as "following what is spontaneous [or 'natural']" (*ziran*), and "taking no action that is contrary to nature . . . letting nature take its own course".[10] These characterisations connect *wu wei* with the issue of estrangement from nature. For the condition of people caught up in the febrile pursuits just identified is one in which living spontaneously and naturally is impossible.

There is a connection too with the idea that people in this condition are, unlike the "genuine persons" of an earlier age, no longer "on the course of the Way" (Z 6). This is because the *dao* itself "follows the way of spontaneity [or naturalness]" (D 25).

The meaning of this remark, and indeed of the notions of spontaneity and *wu wei*, is considered later in this book. But, whatever the precise meaning, the idea is that, in failing to live spontaneously, a person fails to accord with the Way and hence to lead an authentic life. The estrangement from nature of those caught up in the restless pursuit of goals, values, knowledge and self-centred satisfaction is at the same time an estrangement from the *dao*.

4

Estrangement, environmentalism and 'otherness'

A few days ago, I stopped to drink a coffee at a restaurant that overlooks the North Sea towards Lindisfarne (Holy Island). At a nearby table, some bird-watchers were waiting for the tide to go out, so that they could cross over the causeway to the island. Next to them was a group intending to visit the 'Birds of Prey Centre' adjoining the restaurant. Close to the restaurant are some holiday cottages that advertise 'eco-holidays'. On the way to the restaurant, I had passed two garden centres and several allotments.

Bird-watching, wildlife centres, gardening, ecotourism – all these enjoy great popularity today. Are they not evidence of a re-convergence with the natural world – one given voice to in the ubiquitous 'green' rhetoric of our times? Politicians, priests, captains of industry all speak of protecting the natural environment, and references to human beings as 'part of' or 'one with nature' belong to the staple vocabulary of environmental organisations.

So why speak of a contemporary estrangement from the natural world? Estrangement may have been a feature of an earlier and darker period of modernity, but, with the dangers of technology and consumerism now recognised, it is fast disappearing. People's consciences and consciousness have been greened, and we can anticipate a new era of convergence already evident in pursuits such as bird-watching and gardening.

Here, then, is another sceptical challenge to the attempt – by Daoists or anyone else – to explain and reflect on our estrangement. There is, this sceptic urges, little or nothing left to explain or reflect on.

The full response to this challenge is the rest of this book. The following chapters develop an account, in a Daoist key, of a convergent relationship to nature, of a sense in which we are or could be 'at one' with the natural world. Readers must judge for themselves whether they are, by the terms of this account, living in estrangement from the natural world. Whether, for example, their participation in bird-watching and in the green rhetoric of the age marks a victory over estrangement.

Rhetoric and reality

There are reasons, in advance of this account, to doubt that today's enthusiasms and rhetoric contradict the impression of contemporary estrangement.

Arguably, the very loudness of the rhetoric betrays a sense of estrangement. Shouting about humankind's being part of nature may mask a fear that it is nothing of the sort. And, anyway, what does such popular rhetoric amount to exactly? I watched a TV science programme yesterday in which the presenter proclaimed that humans are not separate from other things, since everything belongs to a single spatio-temporal universe. But if this is what 'oneness' with things consists in, then it can certainly coexist with a real feeling of estrangement from other living beings – a feeling which the banal thought that we and they belong to the same universe is unlikely to dispel. An empty rhetoric of convergence, however strident, is insufficient to overcome the impression of estrangement.

And what of the contemporary enthusiasms that are said to mark a new age of convergence? I say something later about gardening and wildlife-watching, and I certainly don't assert that everyone who engages in them is only gesturing at convergence with nature. Still, the way that these activities are often pursued bears the marks of the restless contemporary culture – with its imperatives of achievement, busyness, passion, gratification, acquisition, entertainment and information – described in the previous chapter. If the diagnosis there was accurate, these activities may be considered complicit in a continuing estrangement from nature. The bird-watchers on their way to Holy Island had the appearance – to me, at least – of people on a mission to score well in sightings, especially of birds whose rarity seemingly makes them more valuable. Customers emerging from the immense garden centre I drove past struck me as people for whom the garden is less an opportunity for cooperation with nature than for showcasing the plants and employing the gleaming devices they carried out of this horticultural emporium. These devices would no doubt have irritated Zhuangzi's peasant who resisted new-fangled irrigation contrivances.

One questions, too, whether today's environmental enthusiasms and rhetoric go deep with everyone who professes them. During periods of economic recession, familiar green exhortations to eschew automobiles fall silent, with people instead being urged to buy new vehicles to resuscitate the motor industry. In a radio interview last week, a Scottish wildlife manager made all the right ecological noises about the protection of deer during a long, harsh winter – until it emerged that the real reason for protection was the value of deer as targets for shooters' guns and tourists' cameras. Such examples suggest that, behind a green veil – beneath a 'greenwash' – the primary concern is with the human benefits prioritised in a technological society. Many environmentalist proclamations disguise motives similar to those behind the signs in hotel bathrooms which discourage you, in order to 'save the environment', from having your dirty towels laundered.

Remember, too, that even when the rhetoric is not empty or disingenuous, it coexists in the modern consciousness and conscience with indifference to the lot of the billions of creatures that people like to eat, with acquiescence in the control of 'vermin' by "every inventive, malign, brutal method of destruction",[1] and with other forms of complicity in what J. M. Coetzee called a "crime of stupefying proportions" committed against animals.

In challenging those who deny that our age is one of estrangement from the natural world, there is, however, one line of argument I have not followed.

For writers who equate nature with wilderness, activities such as gardening and organised bird-watching on Holy Island are feeble gestures at convergence with the natural world. An example is the novelist and essayist John Fowles, who castigated 'amateur naturalists', including bird-watchers, for subjecting nature to a calculating inspection and categorisation that obstructs convergence. For him, our separation from nature is curable only through recapturing the "psyche" of our "wild, green-men" ancestors, and re-immersing ourselves, wordlessly and in wonder, in a "green chaos".[2]

I haven't followed this line since it is tendentious both to equate the natural with the wild and to regard wordless wonder as the one authentic relationship to nature. This is not, we will see, the Daoist line. There is nothing Mowgli-like or Tarzanesque in those diminutive figures, in Chinese landscape painting, who represent communion with nature. And, while Daoism takes seriously "the mysterious processes of mind" which, writes Fowles, "correspond" to the processes of nature, it does not identify convergence with wordless, ecstatic absorption in nature.

A fuller response to Fowles, and to this sceptical challenge itself, requires a discussion in later chapters of such notions as wildness and indeed nature itself. The same goes for another sceptical concern to which I now turn.

Nature's 'otherness'

The indictment, a few paragraphs back, of the brutality of vermin control comes from an engaging book, subtitled 'A life with birds', whose author chronicles her close relationship with corvids, especially a rook and a magpie that lived in her home. I, too, briefly recorded my own modest experience of convergence with these birds – a tree-full of which I can see now from my office.

But in a different context or mood, the experience may be more like the one evoked in these lines:

In a bare tree,
Black-cloaked crows
Glare down upon us.
Their soulless eyes glinting,
Growing colder.[3]

Then there are creatures which, in almost any context or mood, seem entirely remote from humanity – crocodiles, say, whose "fascination comes . . . not from their kinship but from their distance from us".[4] Places, too, may fascinate because of, not despite, their alien character – a mountain in Scotland, for example, so "entirely indifferent" to the climber that, as he later wrote, he could feel no "companionship" or "relation" with it.[5]

These are experiences, in Iris Murdoch's striking phrase, of the "sheer alien pointless independent existence"[6] of creatures and natural places – of their "radical alterity"[7] or 'otherness'. They are experiences that an adequate description or perceptive phenomenology of encounters with the natural world must encompass.

But in that case, why assume that estrangement from nature is 'a bad thing', something to be 'overcome' in a re-convergence with nature? Isn't recognition of nature's 'radical alterity' essential to an authentic relationship to nature? For isn't the alternative a deluded anthropomorphism that imputes human features to everything?

There are no instant answers to these questions, which challenge the assumption that estrangement from nature is generally to be regretted. They certainly can't be answered by reciting unexamined slogans to the effect that human beings are also animals, also part of nature. The appropriate response to the challenge is to show that experience of 'otherness' – of creatures and places which offer no 'companionship' – is integral to genuine convergence with nature. Estrangement ('a bad thing') should not be confused with appreciation of radical difference between the human and the non-human ('a good thing'). (Difference, note, not opposition.) The sole alternative to acceptance of estrangement is not, therefore, an anthropomorphic delusion of cosy kinship between the natural and human worlds.

Daoists certainly cannot be accused of anthropomorphic delusion. Three attractive and related themes in the *Zhuangzi* are relevant in this connection.

The story is told of an unfortunate captured bird. "The ruler of Lu was delighted by it, presenting to it a feast replete with all the finest meats and having . . . music performed for it". Soon, however, the bird "started to appear worried and sad, looking around in a daze, not venturing to eat or drink". The moral of the story is the silliness of nourishing a creature which is at home in "deep forests and gliding through rivers", where it feeds on "wiggly things", with "what would nourish oneself" (Z 19, also Z 3). In this and several other stories, people are criticised for attributing to creatures attitudes, beliefs or desires that are confined to human beings.

Then there are the passages where, following on from this point, it is emphasised that other living beings – trees, perhaps, as well as animals – have perspectives of their own. It is reported that Zhuangzi himself never dismissed or ignored other creatures'"views of right and wrong". Interestingly, the text adds that it was because of this that Zhuangzi "never arrogantly separated himself off" from these creatures (Z 33). Recognition of the different perspectives of other creatures is, therefore, a reason *against*, not *for*, speaking of a "separation" from them. This is not to deny, of course, that sometimes it is legitimate to attribute to animals a feeling or attitude that corresponds to a human one. In the absence of evidence to the contrary, one anecdote implies, it is fine to suppose that the fish swimming freely beneath the bridge are *happy* (Z 17).

Finally, and more generally, the *Zhuangzi* speaks against a human bias and partiality that prevents people from seeing other living beings for what they are. Here the point is not simply that partiality is an obstacle to truth. It is an obstacle as well to the proper treatment of animals, trees and other living beings. Guo Xiang explains this well in his commentary on a passage from Chapter 7:

> To allow [creatures or things] to spontaneously grow into being as they will is what it means to be unbiased. When your mind wants to add something to them [to impose an interpretation on them], this is selfish bias. Indulging your bias . . . never produces the life of things . . . [Being] free of any bias leaves all beings intact and complete.

In short, respect for the natural integrity of things – of animals, plants and places – requires abandonment of a partial and anthropomorphic perspective which distorts their nature.

Zhuangzi, in effect, has turned the tables on the sceptic. It is not, as the sceptic maintained, the 'otherness' of nature which entails that we are estranged from it: rather, it is human blindness to 'otherness' which is alienating. To evaluate this response and the one to the earlier sceptic, who questioned the extent of estrangement in contemporary society, attention must turn to notions – especially that of nature – which I've so far been employing casually. How, we need to ask, is nature understood in the Daoist texts?

Nature in Daoism

Attention to the Daoist idea of nature is made more urgent by yet another sceptical challenge that it is important to confront. For what is now challenged is my book's guiding assumption that Daoism really does address the question of an authentic relationship to the natural world.

This sceptic is aware of Daoism's 'green' reputation for adopting friendly and responsible attitudes towards nature, having perhaps read dithyrambic tributes like this one:

> All these frantic last-minute efforts to latch on to some 'new idea' for saving the earth are unnecessary. It's been done for us already – thousands of years ago – by the Taoists. We can drop all that frantic effort and begin following the way of Lao Tzu and Chuang Tzu.[1]

But the sceptic wonders if this reputation is deserved. The worry is that while Daoists have a lot to say about nature, this isn't nature in the relevant sense. In earlier chapters, we heard that, according to Daoism, people should not oppose the workings of nature or attribute to human effort what is nature's doing; that they should respect the natures of different beings and act spontaneously or naturally. But none of this, it is charged, bears on the question of how a person should relate to animals, plants, landscapes and natural environments – to the nature which TV nature programmes are about, which nature writers and natural historians write on; to nature in contrast with culture; to the nature some people yearn for convergence with.

'Nature', in the earlier chapters, variously referred to the material universe as a whole, the general processes called 'laws of nature', the essential characteristics of a thing, and what spontaneous behaviour accords with. Daoist pronouncements on nature in these various senses may be worth heeding but, the sceptic maintains, have no implications for a person's relationship to natural environments and the beings that live in them.

'Nature': some connected senses

Much of this objection is valid. 'Nature' does have several senses, and to speak about it in some of these is not necessarily to discuss the kind that concerns us. And certainly ancient Chinese contained several terms which, in context, may approximately be translated by the word 'nature'. *Tian* (heaven), *tiandi* (heaven-and-earth) and *tianxia* ('all under heaven') sometimes refer to nature-as-a-whole or the general processes of nature; *xing* and *benxing* to the inherent or 'original' nature of things, including 'human nature'; and *jing* to nature in the sense of something's essence. An important term, encountered earlier, is *ziran* (*tzu-jan*), often rendered by 'spontaneous' or 'natural', but more literally by a phrase like 'being so of itself'. There were also various terms for natural landscapes – such as *shansui* and *shanlin*, which are composed out of the characters for mountains, water and forests. Where the aim was to speak of places more or less unaffected by human intervention, terms such as *huangye* ('wilderness expanse') were available.[2]

The sceptic argues that Daoist thinkers, in speaking of, say, *tian* or *ziran*, were not speaking about nature in the relevant, natural environment, sense – and reminds us that there was no Chinese term for nature in that sense. This is quite true. What doesn't follow, though, is the conclusion that the Daoist discourse of *tian*, *ziran* and the rest has no bearing on the issue of an authentic relationship to the world of nature.

It's important to recognise that, while our word 'nature' has several senses, these are not unconnected. It's no accident that we speak both of the laws of nature and of a person's nature. The root of this and related words, such as 'native', is the Latin term for 'born' (*natus*). The term applied originally to the inherent character of something, as in 'lions are aggressive by nature'. The term's use then widened, to refer to whatever develops and changes of its own accord, or in keeping with its own laws – to, in effect, the processes of nature-as-a-whole. These laws of nature were contrasted with the humanly constructed laws by which people govern their actions. With this contrast in place, 'natural' could also be applied to human behaviour that is not contrived, artificial and calculating – to spontaneous behaviour. Finally, 'nature' came to signify, instead of nature-as-a-whole, those segments of it that are comparatively independent of human intervention and control – natural environments and wilderness.

These connections also exist among the different Chinese concepts of nature. In Daoist writing, moreover, the grounding of these concepts in the notion of the *dao* means that there is a further, deeper connection.

The *dao*, announces the *Daodejing*, is "the origin of heaven and earth (*tiandi*)" and, through the processes of heaven and earth, "the mother of the myriad things" (D1). Under the sway of the most general of these processes – the harmonious opposition of *yin* and *yang* – creatures and things are "nourished" and "completed" (D 42, 51). So the *dao* is responsible for nature-as-a-whole and for the natures or essences of individual beings. These are not distinct responsibilities: for it is only through belonging in the matrix of heaven and earth that each being has its nature and is what it is. Since "the Way runs through and connects everything", and "all things give form to one another", then in a sense "all things are one" (Z 22, 23).

The idea – and ideal – of naturalness or spontaneity is also grounded in the *dao*, which, as the origin of everything, is not bound by or acted upon by anything outside of itself. It is *ziran*, 'so of itself'. Nor, as an impersonal source of the world, does it deliberate, contrive, plan or calculate. On both counts, "the *dao* follows the way of spontaneity" (D 25). This is why human beings are "great" and "on the Way" when they live spontaneously and, in addition, "support the [other] myriad creatures in their natural condition" (D 64).

Daoist thinkers may not have had a term for the nature which nature writers write about, but we've recorded in earlier chapters their plea for convergence with nature in this sense and for adopting

appropriate attitudes towards other living beings and their environments. In the light of the above remarks on the *dao* and *ziran*, we can
now see why animals, mountains, water and forests should figure
prominently in the Daoist imagination. It is because nature in this
sense is the domain of naturalness and spontaneity, of the unimpeded
workings of the *dao* – the domain, therefore, to seek convergence with
if human lives are to accord with the *dao*.

This is confirmed by the metaphors Daoists reach for when
describing the lives of men and women who are 'on the Way'. These
lives flow like water and develop in the manner of plants, and they are
simple and undistorted like an uncarved block of wood. There are
many passages where the contrived existence of human beings is contrasted with the spontaneity that prevails in nature. The *Zhuangzi*
compares a horse that, free to graze and gallop, manifests its "true
nature" with another horse which has been broken, branded and bri-
dled. The author writes that this is not "the way to manage the world"
and goes on to describe, by way of contrast, an idyllic age in which "all
creatures lived together, merging their territories into one another".
In those days of "perfect virtue", "people lived together with the birds
and the beasts". Human beings, animals, grasses, trees, marshes and
mountains all existed "unimpeded", so that their inborn natures were
properly realised (Z 9).

Later, texts of 'religious' Daoism took up the theme. The Han
dynasty *Taiping jing* (*Scripture of Great Peace*),[3] for instance, looks back
to a Golden Age, before human beings embarked on insensitive, earth-
gouging construction projects, when people and other living beings
existed in a state of simple and harmonious naturalness.

Later in this chapter it will become clear how, according to
Daoism, an appropriate relationship to natural environments enhances
a person's accord with the *dao*. It will emerge that the need for such a
relationship is implied by the larger Daoist vision in which the
accounts of nature-as-a-whole, the individual natures of things, and
natural or spontaneous behaviour, are located.

That there is this enhancement is the answer to the sceptical challenge mentioned at the beginning of the chapter. Much more plausible than the accusation that Daoism was not concerned with nature in

the sense of the natural environment is the judgement that its primary concern was not with nature *qua* wilderness.

Chinese landscape paintings typically depict places that are, to a degree, 'humanised' – by the presence of buildings, farms, hermitages, boats. The nature whose praises are sung by Tao Qian and Tang poets such as Li Bai (Li Po) is more 'countryside' than wilderness. During the Song dynasty the practice grew of visiting scenic places, to view and picnic or play in them. These *bajing* (literally, 'eight scenes') were not wildernesses, but areas deemed worth visiting because they had been enhanced by human activity, often the temple-building and garden-making of Daoist or Buddhist priests.[4]

There are several reasons why there was no 'wilderness ideal' in ancient China of the kind now embraced by many Western environmentalists. Without the gadgetry, medicines and rescue services on which today's aficionados of the wild can rely, wildernesses must have been dangerous and difficult places to visit. But there are reasons too of a less pragmatic sort. It is sometimes suggested that the Chinese were without this ideal because they rejected the dichotomy between the human and the wild. Reading Tang poetry and viewing Chinese landscape paintings, says Robert Macfarlane, "you encounter an art in which almost no divide exists between nature and the human".[5]

There's a truth in this, but one difficult to articulate ahead of examining, in the next chapter, the notion of the *dao* and its implications for the polarities of ordinary, everyday thought. But Daoists would certainly echo one main theme in Macfarlane's book *The Wild Places*. Wildness, he argues, is nearly everywhere: in a small wood close to a city as much as on a remote mountainside. This is because wildness is a "process . . . continually at work in the world . . . an ongoing organic existence, vigorous and chaotic".[6] He's right. To experience wildness, there is no need to go into a wilderness. In one's garden – underfoot, overhead and all around – wild creatures are doing what wild creatures do, and processes of generation and decay are at work. The garden shed and bird table do not belong to a wilderness, but the behaviour of the birds that perch on top of the shed before flying to the table doesn't differ in essence from that of birds in the deepest jungle.

The point is one that Zhuangzi recognised. The animals that figure in many of his anecdotes – birds, fish, horses – do not live in a wilderness but alongside people in villages and their environs. As we have seen, however, Zhuangzi distinguishes between the behaviour these creatures share with animals in the wild and behaviour that is forced on them by people. For Zhuangzi, we should, as far as possible, allow these creatures their wildness.

A final reason why the Daoist emphasis is not on wilderness is that an authentic relationship to nature should be real, not vicarious. Reading about wildernesses, or viewing images of them on a TV screen, is fine, but hardly in itself a form of meaningful convergence. It is difficult even today - for financial, domestic and other reasons – for people to pop in and out of wilderness areas, and impossible for all but a very few to experience an engaged relationship with a wilderness. Now, Daoists are not speaking only to intrepid explorers, wildlife cameramen, park rangers and desert hermits, but to each of us. The relationship to nature which they urge is one that a fashion photographer, a university lecturer or a plumber might cultivate – a relationship, certainly, from which people are not debarred just because they spend little or no time out there in a wilderness.

Nature as educator

Daoists emphasise the importance of an authentic relationship with nature because it contributes to a life that is in harmony with the Way. It does so because it edifies. Appropriately experienced and engaged with, nature at once educates, enables and invokes the virtues.

Like several ancient literatures, Daoist writings tell Aesopian tales whose purpose is to teach lessons for us humans. The opening chapter of the *Zhuangzi* tells of a cicada and a dove which, in scoffing at a giant bird, only demonstrate the perils of viewing things from narrow, partial perspectives. In a later chapter, the ability of fish not to bump into one another in a crowded pond is a lesson in the frictionless conduct of social life (Z 6).

But nature has a larger educative role than to illustrate a bit of good advice. In the natural world, one experiences processes which, unobstructed by human intervention, are therefore under the sway of heaven-

and-earth, hence of the *dao*. Because of this, aspects of the natural world serve as models for how men and women might enjoy greater harmony with the *dao*. The main model in the *Daodejing* is water, which the text urges people to emulate. Water and plants have been described as 'root metaphors' in Chinese thought,[7] for they are deployed not so much to lend rhetorical colour as to guide thinking. Once water is perceived to be an especially apt expression of the *dao*, meditation on water generates further thoughts on the human condition.

Water has no shape of its own, but takes on that of its container; it flows freely, but typically along a course or channel; agitated water does not reflect its surroundings, whereas still water does; clear water, while it reflects well, is itself hard to see; water does not 'contend', but flows past obstacles towards its destination; water flows downward to lie at the lowest level of a place. From these observations, implications are drawn for the proper conduct of human life. Some of these are not obvious, which suggests that the analogy is doing real work in generating, not just poetically expressing, comparisons between water and human life. Guided by the model, the sage will respond in a supple way to circumstances; maintain stillness and clarity of mind, while recognising the difficulty of describing this state; act in a 'feminine', non-contending manner; and feel no shame in occupying a lowly station in society.

The idea of nature as an instructive model for human conduct is sometimes linked to the development during the Han dynasty of a cosmology of 'correlatives' or 'correspondences'.[8] According to the 'Five Processes' (*wuxing*, literally 'five doings' or 'goings') doctrine, the natural functions of wood and metal, say, were systematically correlated with, for example, political roles. In the second-century BCE work the *Huainanzi*, elaborate parallels were drawn between nature and the human body: sky/head, seasons/limbs, wind/liver, weather/temper, and so on. This cosmology is best regarded as a baroque development of an earlier, simpler vision of a *dao* that courses through and thereby connects heaven, earth, animals and people. Within this vision, flowing water or a growing tree may express qualities which, when embodied by a human being, constitute virtues such as humility, patience and flexibility.

Since one can read or be told about the lessons nature teaches, why is there a need for direct, personal experience of lakes, forests, mountains? Part of the answer is indicated in these lines from a later advocate of nature as educator, William Wordsworth:

> One impulse from a vernal wood
> May teach you more of man,
> Of moral evil and of good,
> Than all the sages can.[9]

Direct acquaintance with nature and its symbols of virtue and vice is simply a more effective teacher than any book or lecture. As a Song dynasty landscape designer in Huzhou wrote, to "moralise people", it is "better to let them enjoy the scenery of the lake than to preach to them".[10] This is not the main reason, however, why to be educated by nature people should experience it for themselves. The most significant education provided by nature is not information, not Aesopian analogues of human foibles, not models from which to draw lessons. Instead, it is – as Plato said all education should be – an 'orientation', a 'turning [of] the mind as a whole', like the turning of an eye from darkness to light. In Robert Macfarlane's words, experience of forests "changes the grain of the mind".[11]

These are not effects that instruction – even from the lips of sages – can bring about. For the change is one in sensibilities, in attunement to the world, and is effected by acquaintance, familiarity, engagement. Sensibilities learned through acquaintance with the rhythms and spontaneous processes of natural life then become available to people when considering the direction of their own lives.

Nature's education of sensibility is illustrated by remarks in the *Zhuangzi* on attitudes towards death. Zhuangzi is sometimes accused of flippancy here – and certainly he was able, on his deathbed, jokingly to chide his followers for proposing a burial that would rob the birds of a meal. "Above ground I'll be eaten by crows and vultures, below by ants and crickets," he exclaims. "Now you want to rob the one to feed the other. Why such favouritism?" (Z 32). But his considered position is that, while one naturally and properly "feels the loss" when a person dies, death is not to be feared or lamented. From an impartial perspective, death is the dispersal of energy which gathered together at birth, and part therefore of a universal process of transformation. Birth and death follow each other like the seasons in a rhythm that is a precondition of life itself. The world is too much an interconnected whole for people to celebrate the "sacred and precious" while lamenting the "foul and the rotten" (Z 22).

These truths, Zhuangzi thinks, are rather obvious, but people fail to internalise them because they do not recognise how continuous human existence is with that of nature at large. Were they to pay close attention to nature – to the numberless creatures "taking shape . . . receiving energy from the yin and yang" and then dissolving – people would not regard themselves as special, discrete entities whose death is something momentous (Z 17). Those with mature experience of natural life appreciate that nature is a "great cauldron" of "creation-transformation" and accept with equanimity their own subjection to this process (Z 6). To accept this is, in effect, to recognise that living in convergence with nature is to live out the truth of things.

Nature and virtue

Experience of nature edifies – brings people closer to the Way – not only through educating but also by invoking the virtues and being an arena for their exercise. Here, I shall be brief, since this is a central theme in several later chapters. It would in any case be hard to elaborate ahead of closer examination, in the following chapters, of the ideas of *dao* and *de*.

Daoist philosophers and poets often contrast living in the countryside with urban life. The main point of the contrast, however, is not that cities are dens of iniquity so corrupting that those who spend their lives there are incapable of goodness. Rather, it's the thought that in urban existence – or in any context dominated by human business, by a restless pursuit of goals, technical knowledge, profit and pleasure – not only are people estranged from nature but are without space in which to exercise certain virtues. It is the thought expressed by Wordsworth in a sonnet which complains that, when we are 'out of tune' with nature, "The world is too much with us; late and soon, / Getting and spending, we lay waste our powers".[12] The poem recalls remarks in the *Daodejing* critical of those who, having abandoned simplicity and modesty, "would gain the world and do something with it", and who are after "profit" and dominion (D 19, 51). "The sage discards . . . the extravagant and the excessive . . . [and] desires to have no desires. He does not value rare treasures." (D 29).

Zhuangzi continues the theme. If people are to return to the *dao*, there must be a "letting go of the world", along with its "entanglements" of "rank, wealth, prestige" and desire (Z 19, 23). When offered by the King of Chu an important official position, Zhuangzi asked the royal emissaries whether they would prefer being a turtle that was "alive and dragging its backside through the mud" to being a sacred, dead turtle kept in a bamboo chest at court. Yes they would, came the reply. Then "get out of here!" said Zhuangzi, "I too will drag my backside through the mud" (Z 17).

The natural world affords an opportunity to 'un-self', to 'let go' of the world of purpose and profit in which people put themselves at the centre. Experience of nature helps you, as one wit put it, to get out of your own way. The opportunity is, to begin with, one for mindfulness of, or attention to, things as they are, independently of their function in the world of everyday human affairs. This world, a Spanish philosopher explained, is a "conjunction of favourable and adverse conditions . . . facilities and difficulties in respect of our aspirations"[13] – a world of 'equipment', of things for our use. Things are what they are – computers, hammers, books – only in relation to these aspirations and purposes.

Since the *dao* has no aspirations, a person emulates it through being "a mirror" of things and responding to them as they are, without "storing" or categorising them in terms of their utility. This 'indifference' or "quiescence" is difficult to maintain except in mindful experience of beings that don't depend, for what they are, on their use by us (Z 7, 13). That is why there is a point to experiencing the 'sheer pointless independent existence', in Murdoch's phrase, of birds, flowers, rivers.

Because the *dao* has no aspirations, it is without partiality. This is why the sage who is "on the Way" will "sort out but does not assess" (Z 2). He distinguishes between things, but without invidiously judging which are better or worse: in this sense, he treats all beings as one. Like the *dao* itself, he deems "no thing . . . more valuable than any other". Again, this is difficult to accomplish in a human world with its relentless focus on the comparative value and utility of objects.

Immersed in experience of nature, on the other hand, a person not only loses the sense of being something special around which the world revolves, but also develops a feel for the "uncontrived inclinations" of other creatures and an appreciation that they, too, have their "own mandates". Only from an arbitrary, partial perspective can these mandates be rejected as trivial in relation to human purposes (Z 14, 17). With respect for the integrity of other living beings, there develops, then, another virtue – humility. For, while sages do not make invidious comparisons between the worth of human beings and other creatures, they recognise that in the scheme of things – and from the perspective of the *dao* – "the human realm is like the tip of a hair on the body of a horse" (Z 17).

So far, the virtues for whose exercise nature provides an opportunity have been, in a sense, negative. The opportunity is for no longer being partial, for being 'disinterested', for not overrating the importance of one's own goals and perspectives, for 'silencing the will'. It is important, however, to appreciate that, for the Daoist, nature is also a theatre for the exercise of the 'positive' virtues of spontaneity. If nature is a place for self-overcoming, it is also one for self-expression, élan, physical and psychic vitality, and freedom. As a great Tang painter and poet expressed it:

> I can't be bothered with all the affairs of the world [. . .]
> I'm simply concerned to go back to my old forest home,
> Where the wind of the pines loosens the belt of my gown
> And the mountain moon shines down on the zither I play.
> You ask what the principle is for achieving the Way –
> A fisherman's song going into the deep river bank.[14]

In the famous 'Preface to a book of poems composed at the Orchid Pavilion',[15] the fourth-century-CE calligrapher Wang Xizhi relates how, away from the town and acutely aware of the "manifold riches of the earth", the eyes of the poets wandered freely, with their hearts "rambling" along with them.

Rambling or roaming (*yu*) is an important theme in the *Zhuangzi*. It is no accident that this metaphor for pliancy and fluidity of mind is drawn from an activity pursued in natural environments. For it is here, liberated from conventions and the clamour of human affairs, that people can be spontaneous. Nor is it an accident that the metaphor is taken from a physical activity. You should "revere your own body", asserts the *Daodejing*, and people "who care for their bodies as if they were the entire world can be entrusted with the world" (D 13). From the beginning, Daoism, like most ancient philosophies, emphasised bodily discipline and health. This was to become a paramount concern in 'religious' Daoism. But in the *Zhuangzi* there were already passages combining the themes of freedom, spontaneity, responsiveness, balance of mind and body, and psychic and bodily vitality. In one passage (Z 19), the person who maintains balance and vitality is said to have "become a helper of heaven" and hence to be in accordance with the Way. It is crucial to keep in mind, if our perspective is to be a Daoist one, the grounding in the *dao* of the virtues we have been discussing. The idea

A detail from 'Gathering at the Orchid Pavilion', Qian Gu.
© Metropolitan Museum of Art / Art Resource / Scala, Florence

that nature edifies is, after all, found in several traditions of thought that owe nothing to Daoism: in the romanticism of Rousseau and Wordsworth, for example.

The distinctively Daoist thought is that, in an authentic relationship to nature, exercise of these virtues is grounded in a certain wisdom. Unless infused with this wisdom, it is not real virtue. Respect for the integrity of other creatures, for example, is not genuinely virtuous when severed from this wisdom. The wisdom in question is knowledge of the *dao* and of the dependence upon it of everything, us included. It's not that a life led in an appropriate relationship with nature is constantly punctuated by explicit philosophical thoughts about the *dao*, but, for this to be the relationship advocated by Daoists, the life must manifest understanding of the *dao*. It is time, therefore, to address the question 'What is the *dao*?'

6

On the Way (1):
dao, world and unity

We have reached the point where further discussion of convergence with nature requires closer attention to the pivotal notions of *dao* and *de*, which give to the Daoist approach its distinctive character. In this and the next chapter I offer an account of what it is to be 'on the Way', to be in harmony or accord with the *dao*.

Dao, God, nature and nothing

'*Dao*' is variously translated as 'way', 'course', 'path' and 'road' – but also, in its verbal form, as 'to lead' or 'to cut a path or channel'. It can also mean 'to teach, tell or explain' and refer to a teaching or discourse. (In his translation of the first line of the *Daodejing*, Alan Watts neatly exploited this ambiguity: "The course that can be discoursed is not the eternal course.") It will be helpful to bear in mind these further uses of '*dao*'.

Talk of ways or courses for human beings to follow was pervasive in classical Chinese texts. A way was usually a human practice – fishing, say, or governing a country – as it ought to be, a practice skilfully conducted. In Confucian texts, the reference was sometimes broader – to the consummate conduct of a life in keeping with the wisdom of one's ancestors. There was talk, too, of the way of heaven – of the natural order that, in its regularity and reliability, had a lesson for human conduct.

In the Daoist texts, the notion of *dao* becomes at once more fundamental and more recondite. Its primary reference is not to human conduct, but to a Way with which all human practice should accord.

Dao is no longer simply the regular course of heaven or nature, but the very source of heaven, nature and the myriad things. This is the resounding message of the *Daodejing*, where *dao* is said to "beget" or "be the mother of all things", to "exist before heaven and earth", both of which "follow" or "model" themselves on *dao* – as indeed we should too (D 25). The texts make it clear, too, that while we know that there is this source of all things, little or nothing of a literal kind can be said about it. *Dao* cannot be "discoursed": it is an "enigma", a "mystery", "the deepest and most profound" (D 1). Since it is only objects or beings that can be described, their "root" or source – not itself an object – cannot be (Z 25).

Already the value of bearing in mind the verbal, dynamic form of '*dao*' is emerging. *Dao* is not ineffable because it is a thing too grand for language to depict. Rather, it is not a thing or object at all. The question 'What is the *dao*?' is, in fact, a misleading one, for it suggests that *dao* is a special being or object. To help avoid this suggestion – and in keeping with Chinese grammar – I am now omitting the definite article before '*dao*'.

The temptation to regard *dao* as a very special being was succumbed to by translators of an earlier generation,[1] who urged that *dao* could be identified with God, albeit a more 'abstract' one than the biblical God. While there may be reason to regard *dao* as it figures in later, 'religious' Daoism as a "cosmic power which creates the universe",[2] this is not *dao* as presented in the classic texts. The *Daodejing* asserts that, if there is a 'supreme spirit' or God (*di*), this was *preceded* by *dao* (D 4). *Dao* is the source of God, if He exists, just as it is of every other being. Zhuangzi explains that *dao* is not a "something [some *thing*] which causes" or creates: it is not a "substance", as God is traditionally conceived to be (Z 25). Zhuangzi's remark suggests, too, that it would be wrong to identify *dao* with any "transcendent" being deemed to be separate from the world, as its alleged "cause" or "creator" would have to be. (More on this point later in the chapter.)

It is understandable that, in recoil from the theistic construal of *dao*, later commentators veer towards much flatter, downbeat interpretations – a solidly 'naturalistic' one, for example. In this view, *dao* is simply "the universal law that governs the motion and change of nature".[3] But it is hard to reconcile this view with passages in which *dao* is said to "give rise to" the vital forces of nature, *yin* and *yang*, and nature or heaven is alleged to "arise from what is not there", from what lacks substance (*dao*, in other words) (D 42, 40).

While '*dao*' is sometimes used interchangeably with 'heaven' or 'nature', a more judicious view than the naturalistic one is that of the third-century BCE author Hanfeizi (Han Fei Tzu), the leading figure in a tough-minded school of political philosophers known as 'the Legalists'. Hanfeizi writes:

> *Dao* is that by which all things become what they are ... with which all principles (*li*) are commensurable. Principles are patterns (*wen*) according to which all things come into being, and *dao* is the course of their being.[4]

This perceptive passage nicely exposes the dual use of '*dao*' as a name for the source of all things – 'that by which' they become what they are – and as a term for the general processes or patterns of the natural world. The naturalist's mistake is to ignore the first, and distinctively Daoist, of these senses.

A second interpretation – a 'nihilistic' one – also in recoil from the theological reading, was first proposed by Guo Xiang. He picks up on the book's denial that *dao* is a being or entity. If it is a 'non-being', he argues, the claim that everything is produced by *dao* can only mean that it is produced by nothing. In other words, things have no cause or source, since "each thing self-generates, without recourse to anything that goes beyond itself".[5] The Daoist message, in this view, is that of the world's radical, ungrounded contingency. If *dao* is what human beings should follow, this can only be *dao* in the sense, noted above, of a *teaching*.

Guo Xiang's interpretation is ingenious, but hard to reconcile with the texts. The very passage on which he draws in rejecting *dao* as a 'thing' that creates the world also denies that *dao* is a 'nothing'. "The Way cannot be treated as Something, or as Nothing either", says Zhuangzi: neither characterisation is adequate to *dao* (Z 25). The interpretation does no justice, either, to remarks in the *Daodejing* where *dao* is emphatically said to be the source of things – "something undifferentiated and all-embracing" which precedes heaven, earth and the myriad things (D 25). Nor can the *dao* that everything follows or should follow always be construed simply as a teaching or discourse. When heaven "follows the way of the *dao*" (D 25), it is not following a teaching, and Laozi is explicit that his own words or teachings have "their own source" or "ancestor", namely *dao* (D 70).

The naturalistic and nihilistic reactions to the equation of *dao* with God are understandable. But they are also unnecessary. To eschew a divine or transcendent *dao*, there is no need to reduce *dao* to natural laws or to nothing. We should consider the possibility of a source of the world which is distinct from the transcendent creator of Western theology and metaphysics.

Dao, experience and world

The following account of *dao* isn't explicitly articulated in the classic texts, but it is implied by crucial claims of Zhuangzi's and it explains and illuminates salient features attributed to *dao*. My account is, in effect, a reconstruction – one in a Daoist key, even if it doesn't exactly correspond to anything stated in the classics.

Zhuangzi, in modern philosophical parlance, was a 'perspectivist'. For him (as for Friedrich Nietzsche, who gave the term philosophical currency), no judgement or belief is true or false, right or wrong, except relative to a perspective. Relative, that is, to a way of experiencing, conceptualising and describing the world. This is the point of such remarks as "What is It is also Other, what is Other is also It. There they say 'That's it, that's not' from one point of view, here we say 'That's it, that's not' from another point of view." Or: "Things are so by being called so . . . Each thing has some place [perspective] from which it can be affirmed as thus and so" (Z 2). Independently of perspective, a beam is no different from a pillar; a hag no different from a beauty.

Different perspectives, moreover, abound. Not only are there many actual or possible human perspectives, but those of other creatures too. Zhuangzi, as we saw in Chapter 4, refused to dismiss other creatures' "views of right and wrong" (Z 33). These perspectives reflect the interests, desires, natures and situations of the different people or creatures whose perspectives they are. It is among the "essentials" or "characteristic inclinations" of human beings, for example, to judge things according to "likes and dislikes" (Z 5).

It is important to understand that, for Zhuangzi – as for Nietzsche – the point is not that we lack *knowledge* as to which perspective correctly mirrors reality. The point is the more radical one that it is senseless to regard any particular perspective as correct. There can be no 'fixity' or 'constancy' to the ways in which the world may be divided up and described; no external measure for the formation or dissolution of conceptual schemes. From the perspective of each creature, some things are more valuable than others, but when examined in relation to *dao*, which has no perspective, none has more value than another (Z 17). By considering the perspectives of creatures, such as insects and fish, which are strikingly unlike human beings, Zhuangzi – again anticipating Nietzsche – emphasises how parochial or anthropocentric it is to imagine that all perspectives must be similar to our own.

Since it is senseless to regard any perspective as corresponding to reality, Zhuangzi is not critical of people for making 'merely' perspectival judgements. On the contrary, these have a practical use in everyday life, and one should respect both 'the everyday function of each thing' and everyday speech. This is what Zhuangzi calls giving things and words their "lodging-places in the usual" (Z 2). Zhuangzi is critical, however, of people who consider that "for every name . . . there turns out to be a substantial reality" (Z 23). People, in other words, who wrongly suppose that a statement can be *more* than a useful communicative tool, and can be true in any sense other than successfully guiding actions and facilitating social interaction.[6]

It is because the senses of words are inseparable from their practical use in social life that *dao* is ineffable. To be sure, *dao* may be evoked by words used in figurative, poetic ways, as when it is compared to water:

> The great *dao* flows everywhere [. . .]
> All things rely on it for existence,
> And never does it turn away from them [. . .]
> It preserves and nourishes all things,
> But it does not claim to be master over them. (D 34)

Dao cannot, however, be the object of literal description, since it is not an object within the world of experience, and not accessible from any practice-based perspective. Description of *dao* would, impossibly, require language to break free of its moorings in social practice – to "go on holiday", as Ludwig Wittgenstein put it.[7]

There is a further crucial implication of perspectivism for the understanding of *dao*. It is becoming apparent that the question addressed in this chapter about the nature of *dao* is essentially a question about experience – about the ways of perceiving, understanding and describing that constitute perspectives. This does not mean that the question is not, after all, about the 'origin' of the world and the myriad objects – but it does mean that it is about the origin of the world *as* experienced, of things as they are *for* us and other creatures with points of view. For Zhuangzi, there is not experience *and*, as a separate domain, the world. For no sense attaches to the idea of a world – of a structured, determinate array of things – independent of all perspective.

Dao may be understood as the condition for all experience – and hence for worlds as experienced. A perspective is itself a way in which the world is experienced or becomes present for us or other creatures. So we might call *dao* "the Way that gives all ways"[8] or "the 'origin' of presence".[9] Recalling the Daoist predilection for aquatic imagery, we might name it the source or well-spring – even the opening up of channels – that enables experience to flow.

This characterisation of *dao* fits with, and helps to explain, various aspects of *dao* remarked on in the classic texts.

First, there is *dao*'s 'gradualism'. Older translations of the first line of the *Daodejing* often render 'the *dao* that cannot be spoken of' as 'the eternal *dao*' – but recent commentators prefer 'constant' to 'eternal'. For the point of the line is not that, like God, *dao* exists for ever, but that the working of *dao* is constant, not a one-off feat as in *Genesis*. As Zhuangzi puts it, *dao* "gives forth continuously" (Z 17). This is what we would expect him to say if, as I propose, *dao* is the ongoing giver – the constant well-spring – of ways of experiencing the world that are continually forming and dissolving.

Next, we are better able to appreciate Hanfeizi's insight into the 'dual use' of '*dao*' to refer to "that by which all things become what they are" and also to the general 'principles' or 'patterns' of the natural world.

The connection between the uses is this: 'constant' *dao* is the fundamental condition for all experience, but, in order for experience to be possible, certain more particular conditions must obtain. These conditions are the 'patterns' that constitute *dao* as the general principles of nature.

An important theme in the *Daodejing* is the process whereby *dao* "takes from what has excess and augments what is deficient" (D 77) and how through the cooperative tension between *yin* and *yang* it guarantees a level of harmony in the world (D 42). The point here is that, in the absence of harmony and regularity, experience of a world would be impossible. For things to be present to experience, there must be sufficient order among our perceptions for them to be recognised as perceptions of, say, bells or dogs. Pattern, harmony and regularity, therefore, are conditions for experience grounded in that *Ur*-condition or well-spring of experience, 'constant' *dao*.

Third, we can now understand the ineffability of *dao* in its proper context. To do so, it is useful to recall Guo Xiang's characterisation of *dao* as 'non-being' or 'nothing'. This, I explained, was incompatible with references to *dao* as 'begetting' or being a 'well-spring' of all things. On the other hand, Guo Xiang's commentary is salutary in emphasising that *dao* is not itself a being and has no form or structure of its own. How could it have, given that it is the condition of each object or being having a form? But, in that case, how could *dao* be described, since something must have a form in order to be a describable object of experience?

The *Zhuangzi* makes the point explicit: since "what forms forms has no form", *dao* "cannot be spoken" and "corresponds to no name" (Z 22). *Dao* is ineffable not because it is a being too stupendous for words to do justice to, but because it is not a being at all: instead, it is the condition or well-spring of all experience of things, a "giving" of perspectives and their worlds. If the idea of things depending on what is not a thing sounds odd, it is perhaps helpful to think of the metaphors of the wheel and the jar in the *Daodejing*. The wheel revolves around an empty hub; the jar needs the empty space contained by the clay. "Only by relying on what is not there", therefore, do such things have a use. Wheels and jars, one might say, require the absence of something – and things at large depend on a source that cannot be a thing, on what "has no substance" (D11).[10]

Finally, the proposed interpretation of *dao* illuminates a very prominent theme in Daoist writings – that of holism, of unity. This theme is of special interest in a book concerned with human beings' convergence with the natural world, and deserves a section of its own.

Self, world and the unity of things

Daoism has been described, with justice, as hostile to dualisms of a kind that have been prominent in Western thought, and I want to articulate its hostility to two of these before unpacking the gnomic claim that "the myriad things are one" (Z 22).

Dao is the source – the 'giving' or 'opening up' – of ways of experiencing the world. Left like that, the proposal might suggest that a sharp distinction exists between *dao* and the world, and between the world and the subjects who experience it. But this is not the intention at all, for the Daoist rejects the dualisms both of source and world and of selves and world. Let me begin with the second of these.

"Heaven and earth were born together with me, and the myriad things and I are one" (Z 2). This is a dramatic rejection of a dualism of self and world. The reason behind it is indicated earlier in the same chapter, when Zhuangzi writes that "without *that* [the world] there would be no me ... but then again without *me* there would be nothing selected out from it all". The point, then, is not that a self is identical with the things it encounters, but that they are co-dependent: there could be no selves or subjects except in relation to a world, and no world except in relation to subjects.

This important point is implied by Daoist perspectivism. Things have their identity – are 'selected out' from the world – in and through ways of experiencing them. Take away the perspectives from which things are experienced, and there would be no things at all. Nothing could show up as this rather than that object. As for the beings which experience a world, these are no more independent of experience, of perspective, than anything else is. In effect, I am a particular channel of experience – a certain route through a world of experience – and nothing more. If so, my existence in the absence of a world I experience is unthinkable – like the existence of a stream in the absence of a landscape to flow through.

As many remarks in the *Zhuangzi* attest, a creature's identity transforms along with transformations in the world it experiences, its life a continuously changing flow (Z 6). Our present tendency to regard a human being as the same person throughout a lifetime may be convenient, but that is all. Nothing rules out adopting a different convention – that, say, of regarding someone whose life is frequently and strikingly transformed as a sequence of different, though related, persons.

To emphasise how a person's identity changes within the "great furnace of transformation" may be the purpose of the famous story of Zhuangzi's dreaming that he is a butterfly. On waking up, he wonders whether he "had been dreaming he was a butterfly, or if a butterfly was now dreaming it was" him (Z 2). This tale is usually taken as making the sceptical point that one cannot really distinguish between dream and reality. But the story makes better sense as suggesting that Zhuangzi would have become a butterfly if his experience changed into the kind butterflies have. The final words of the story, after all, are "this is what we call the transformation of one thing into another" (Z 2). Zhuangzi and the butterfly are each flowing and shifting channels of experience, of the world's presencing. They are not substances or selves with an identity and reality detachable from their courses of experience.

If there is no dualism of self and world, nor is there a dualism of world and *dao*. "The Way", announces the *Neiye*, "is not separated from us ... [it] fills the entire world." Implied here is a rejection of the theistic interpretation of *dao*. God, in the Abrahamic religions, exists independently of the world: the creation of a world was His choice, not something written into His very nature. He might have existed – and, before the creation, did exist – in the absence of a world. Matters are different with *dao*. As the source or well-spring of ways of experience – and hence of the world – *dao* has no being separate from these ways.

The point is explicit in the *Zhuangzi* (Z 22): "That which makes beings beings is not separated from beings by any border." As the source of all borders or distinctions among things, as that which "fills and empties beings", *dao* is not itself a being distinct from the world. Not even notionally can *dao* be imagined in the absence of the things it "gives", of its presencing as a world of experience. One might as well try to imagine the source of a river in the absence of the river, or of the emptying cloud in the absence of the raindrops that fall from it.

Rejection of the dualisms of self and world, and of *dao* and world, is an important aspect of the 'holistic' character of Daoism, of its emphasis on 'unity'. But there is a further aspect especially relevant to human beings' convergence with nature. This is the unity of the world itself, dramatically expressed in the words "the myriad things are one" (Z 22). The idea of the unity of things was prominent in ancient Chinese thought generally, for example in the *Yijing* (*I Ching*, 'The Book of Changes'). But it is important, before going any further, to avoid certain misunderstandings of this idea as developed in Daoist texts.

To begin with, the thought is not that differences between things are illusory. On the contrary, it is made clear that a sage is someone who "sorts things out" and – despite a sense for "the oneness of heaven" – "separates each passing transformation from the rest" (Z 6). The mistake is not to distinguish things, but to consider these distinctions to be objective, to be independent of perspective. In the 'Inner Chapters' of the *Zhuangzi*, in fact, one does not meet with the claim that all things are one, only with the assertion that the sage *treats* them as one by refusing to reify the distinctions between them.

Second, the Daoist idea of unity has little to do with the hypothesis of modern theoretical physics that, at the subatomic level, there exists interdependence among fundamental particles. I mention this since some authors, such as Fritjof Capra and Thich Nhat Han, claim to find this hypothesis anticipated in Daoism. But Daoist unity, as will shortly emerge, is discernible at the level of ordinary experience, and is revealed by mindful attention to things, not by theoretical physics.

If Daoist holism is not the interdependence spoken of by physicists, nor, finally, is it the 'oneness' or 'interbeing' eulogised in some 'New Age' and 'deep ecological' literature. There is nothing in the classic texts to encourage an image of the world as a single 'Great Self' of which all things, ourselves included, are mere aspects. A world of experience is, in a sense, a whole, but not one akin to a single stuff or sacred being into which each thing and creature dissolves like a marshmallow.

In contrast to New Age utterances about the One, Daoist remarks on unity are often making a modest point. In an early commentary on the *Daodejing*, for example, Wang Bi says that all things "in the final analysis are one" on the grounds, simply, that they have a common origin.[11] This makes for a thin conception of unity – as does the frequent suggestion that there is unity because things 'fit together' in some way. Stemming from the same source, or being structurally related to one another, is not as such a strong and interesting form of unity.

"The myriad things are one" becomes a much more interesting statement when taken in its context. The words are immediately followed by the remark that, while people oppose the beautiful and sacred to the odious and rotten, these opposites "transform" into one another (Z 22). This remark recalls the perspectivist denial of fixed, objective distinctions among things and properties. Ordinarily, we oppose a beam to a pillar, a hag to a beauty, but *dao* "opens them into one another, connecting them to form a oneness" (Z 2).

These apparently strange remarks fall into place when we recall that things belong to a world of experience, one viewed from a certain perspective. Their point, then, is that experience is not atomistic. Items of experience – beams, pillars, beauty, ugliness, the sacred and the odious – are what they are only in virtue of their relationships to one another in a great web of experience. No human face could be experienced as beautiful except in contrast with ugly ones, and on the understanding, moreover, that it too might become ugly. Beams and pillars are distinguished only within structures of experience shaped by activities such as building.

Even something as simple as the colour red or the note 'Middle C' cannot be recognised except through its similarities with and differences from other colours or notes. Like the colour spectrum or a musical scale, the world is a whole within which items figure as individual things, creatures or features only through occupying particular niches in the web of experience. The best analogy, perhaps, is with a language. A language is not a collection of atomic words and meanings, since words have their meanings only though their connections and contrasts with other words. Words, like items of experience, have sense and identity only in relation to a whole to which they belong. What is true of words is also true of things: to recall Zhuangzi's remark, all beings – beams, pillars, lepers, beautiful women, strange and grotesque things – "open up into one another" and thereby "form a oneness".

This dimension of Daoist holism will become clearer as we turn, in the next chapter, to the second of the most central concepts of Daoism: *de*.

On the Way (2): *de*, virtues and sages

In 1973 archaeologists discovered, in a second-century BCE tomb at Mawangdui in Hunan Province, two silk editions of the *Daodejing*. In these editions, the familiar order of the two parts of the work is reversed, with what is traditionally regarded as the second part, the *dejing* (Chapters 38–81), placed before the *daojing* (Chapters 1–37). The implication is that, at least for the compilers of the silk editions, the topic of *de* was of no less importance than that of *dao*. It's worth noting, in this connection, that the original title given to Daoist thinkers, by a Han dynasty historian, was 'the school of *dao* and *de*'. Maybe 'Daode-ism' would be a more just label than plain 'Daoism'.

In this chapter, I discuss *de*, relating it to *dao* and to the virtuous sage who is 'on the Way'.

De and the myriad things

Like '*dao*', the term '*de*' has been variously translated. Its renderings include 'power', 'disposition', 'excellence', 'essence', 'charisma' and 'aura'. Most often, it is rendered by 'virtue', usually with the warning that this refers less to moral goodness than to virtue in the medieval sense of something's or someone's inherent capacity to produce certain effects.

This may make it sound as if '*de*' is ambiguous, but those who employed the term would have recognised close connections between the senses just noted. As, indeed, did medieval and Renaissance speakers in the case of 'virtue'. For Chinese readers, as for Quattrocento Italians, it was no accident that a single term, '*de*' or '*virtù*', could simultaneously indicate a person's power, moral character and charisma – since some-one endowed with *de* or *virtù* exerts a powerful influence on others, partly through the inherent character to which his comportment bears witness. Nor was it a linguistic accident that the term could simultane-ously convey a person or thing's excellence, essence, disposition and integrity. A particular animal, say, is only a good example of its kind when it tends to behave in accordance with its essential nature – a nature that gives it its distinctive integrity.

De in its central sense, from which connecting lines can be drawn to the other senses just mentioned, is what makes a particular being an exemplary member of its kind. This is why the *de* of a creature is spoken of as "completing" or "perfecting" it, and as something to "honour" (D 51). The source of all things is *dao*, and what enables any of these to become 'complete' – to be an exemplar of its kind – is its *de*. Something may be, say, a tiger or a tree, but – like a toothless, crippled tiger, or a withered tree – fail to be a 'perfected' being of its kind. (Human beings can fail to manifest *de* in an additional way, as we'll see in the next section of this chapter.)

The idea here goes back to a work traditionally attributed to Con-fucius, *The Doctrine of the Mean* (*Zhong-yong*), where the interesting claim is made that 'sincerity' (*cheng*) – or better, perhaps, 'authenticity' – is what "completes a thing" by conferring upon it its genuine, authentic nature, the characteristic 'excellence' of things of its kind. The work speaks too of how 'sincerity', in enabling something to develop its nature, also enables it to "develop the nature of all things".[1] This returns us to the issue of the unity of things, which, as we saw in the last chapter, was an important aspect of the world whose source is *dao*.

Arguments as to which is the primary Daoist concept, *dao* or *de*, are misleading, since both play essential roles in the explanation of things. "*Dao* is that by which [things] come to be, and *de* is that by which they are what they are", in one commentator's words.[2] *Dao*, says Zhuangzi (Z 23), is "the opening out and arraying of *de*", and hence of the beings whose *de* is their capacity to function properly.

This function, crucially, is not something an individual being could perform in isolation from others. *De* is a deeply relational notion. Elaborating on the claim that 'the myriad things are one', Zhuangzi writes that such is the harmony among the "virtues" or "powers" of things – eyes and ears, for example – that their "functions" cannot really be "told apart" (Z 5). For any one thing to perform its function, it must respond to other things, just as they must to it.

It is because of this 'responsive cohesion'[3] among virtues or powers that the myriad things constitute a unity. It is impossible to experience something as an authentically functioning being of its kind – to experience its *de* – without appreciating its place in a vast web of experience. Employing the helpful model of the holograph, two modern commentators[4] speak of a thing's *de* as a particular 'focus' in the 'field' of the world that is 'given' by *dao*. Each thing contains the world, as it were – or, less paradoxically, experience of any one thing refers us, ultimately, to every other thing. Once we begin imaginatively to 'roam', to use Zhuangzi's expression, from one *de* to another, we end up traversing the world as a whole.

'Profound *de*' and human virtues

The notion of *de*, then, is inseparable from the Daoist conception of the world, for this is a world of experience whose unity is assured through the 'responsive cohesion' of the *de* of the myriad things.

The main concern in Daoist writings, however, is not *de* in general, but the *de* of human beings in particular. There are two large differences between the *de* of things and of people. The first is that, unlike animals, plants and minerals, human beings have largely forfeited their *de*. Their lives fail to realise their true human potential and so fail to accord with the Way. If the *de* of a tiger is degraded – through disease, age or accident – this is not the fault of the tiger. Matters are different in the case of human beings. Whereas, for example, it is the Way of heaven to "take from what has excess and give to what is deficient", it is common human practice in our unjust world to do the opposite. This is one among many reasons that so few people "have the Way" (D 77). In Chapter 3, I mentioned several ways in which, according to Daoist texts, human beings have abdicated from guidance by *dao* and therefore betrayed their *de*. A 'lust after knowledge'; the erection of artificial systems of rules; the frenzied pursuit of goals – through all of this and more, most men and women fail to cohere responsively with the world and with each other.

The *de* of human beings is something they should try to reclaim and foster, and is therefore virtue in an ethically charged sense, and not simply a power or disposition. The 'honour' due to a being on account of its *de* is one that a person has to earn.

The second distinctive feature of human *de* is that it involves understanding of one's appropriate place and function in the world, and hence an understanding of *dao* as the 'giver' of world. This is true, at any rate, of what the *Daodejing* refers to as 'profound *de*' (*xuande*). This 'profound' virtue requires – on the part of a good ruler, for example – knowledge of a 'principle' or 'standard'. This is why:

> Profound *de* is deep and far-reaching;
> It returns to the origin with all things,
> And then leads to the great naturalness. (D 65)

A detail from 'Fisherman', Wu Zhen. This painting illustrates the unintrusive, uncomplicated engagement with nature that Daoism recommends.
© Freer Gallery of Art, Smithsonian Institution, Washington, D.C.

It is important not to misconstrue this requirement for knowledge. The demand is not for explicit, intellectual assent to philosophical truths about *dao* and *de*. On the contrary, we have already encountered Daoism's suspicion of intellect and its insistence on the limits of what can be explicitly articulated. The sage, after all, "spreads his understanding through wordless teaching" (D 2), and practices a "fasting of the mind" and a "sitting and forgetting" (Z 4, 6).

These strictures against intellect and language contrast with admiration for the understanding manifest in the practical skills of the cooks, fishermen, ferrymen and craftsmen who figure in the *Zhuangzi*. In support of the contention that "knowers do not say and sayers do not know", a wheelwright unfavourably compares a Duke's book learning – "reading the dregs of the men of old" – with his own practical understanding. For example, he uses a chisel "not too slow, not

too fast: I feel it in the hand and respond from the heart, the mouth cannot put it into words, there is a knack in it ..." (Z 13). A hunchback who catches cicadas and a maker of buckles are both said to "have the Way" – not because they are "clever", but in virtue of a focused concentration on their work and an easy responsiveness to the materials they work with (Z 19, 22).

What such anecdotes suggest is that the understanding or wisdom that belongs to 'profound *de*' – to being 'on the Way' – is deeply implicit, something 'thickened' through disciplined practices. Rarely, if ever, made explicit by the people who have it, this understanding informs and guides lives that realise the authentic potential of human beings.

Daoist virtues have been encountered several times in this book, especially in Chapter 5 when discussing the edifying influence of experience of nature. This connection between Daoist virtues and a person's relationship to nature will be revisited, in some detail, in later chapters. The question which now concerns us is the relationship between these virtues and *dao*. There is 'profound *de*' when virtue displays implicit understanding of *dao*. But why is that? Why is knowledge of *dao* primarily registered in humility, simplicity and other Daoist virtues, and in a certain ethical tone a life may have?

It is possible to pair off this or that Daoist virtue with some aspect of *dao*, for one can see how such-and-such a virtue corresponds to an understanding of some dimension of *dao*. For example, a sense of our dependence upon *dao* might register as a rejection of hubris; as an embrace of humility. Recognition that *dao* is the source of many perspectives, none of which could uniquely mirror reality, may induce a reticence in judgement, an impartiality appropriate to realising that "nothing can be definitively called worthy or unworthy" (Z 72). Again, appreciation that *dao* works through giving each thing its *de*, a function in a harmonious world of 'responsive cohesion', may inspire respect for a thing's integrity, for the particular place it occupies in the world.

These pairings of particular virtues with elements in the understanding of *dao* are real and important. But it would be good to get a more general feel for how a person's life as a whole might be one of 'profound *de*', through its harmony with a vision of *dao*. What, I want to ask, would the *tone* or *style* of a life 'on the Way' be like? Let's listen to what the texts say.

The *Daodejing* enjoins a person to "attain tenuousness" or "emptiness", to preserve "integrity", "tranquility" and a steady "constancy"
throughout life (D 16). Such a person attains to "enlightenment and
wisdom", displaying an "all-embracing impartiality" that places the
person "at one with the *dao*". Later, we hear that the enlightened
person of constancy and "balance" does not "force things" or try to
control "the vital energies" (*qi*). Rigid people who force things in a
given direction live "contrary to the *dao*" (D 55).

In the *Zhuangzi*, too, we are enjoined to "follow along" and to
resist "trying to add anything to the process of life" by manipulating it
according to our "likes and dislikes" (Z 5). In Chapter 7, Liezi is praised
for returning to a life of simplicity, of "unhewn blockishness", and a
verse then advises against preoccupation with having "a good name",
being a "repository of plans and schemes", attempting to control
affairs, and imposing one's own understanding on things. Instead,
Zhuangzi continues, "use your mind like a mirror", respond to things
instead of controlling them, keep yourself pliable without concentration on gain, "identify with the limitless" and "roam" without any
fixed destination.

A later chapter tells us to ignore what we can do nothing about,
but to keep the body intact and maintain vitality. This requires us to
"liberate" the body from "always having to be doing something", and
this in turn requires us to "let go of the world" and "abandon worldly
ambitions". People who succeed in doing this are then "free of entanglements", hence balanced and able to renew life, to be "reborn . . . side
by side with what is other" than themselves. Nothing, we read, can
"really harm" the sage who lives according to this dispensation. With
his body "intact" and "vitality restored", he is, in effect, "one with
heaven" (Z 19).

Here, finally, is a passage from Guo Xiang's commentary on the
Zhuangzi which invokes the familiar analogy of life with water:

> Now, water is forever free of intentions, handing itself over to
> follow external things, so whether flowing or still . . . it is
> always like the reservoir, never losing its stillness and silence.
> When the Consummate Person puts it [his 'reservoir'] to use,

he flows forth. When he lets go of it, he is still. . . . [He] is forever undisturbed and satisfied, moored in his forgetting of all deliberate action.[5]

Rather than laboriously comment on these passages, I want to sketch a picture they conjure up – a portrait of the Daoist sage or 'consummate' person, who has 'profound *de*' and is 'on the Way'.[6]

The Daoist sage

What follows is indeed only a sketch. Only lightly touched in, for example, is a view of the sage's convergent relationship to natural environments – for this relationship is the theme of the remaining chapters. Within the sketch, I make a rough, but useful, distinction between the *comportment* of sages and their *attunement* to things. Under the first heading come the sage's ways of behaving, 'lifestyle' and treatment of others. Under the second come the prevailing moods, outlooks and attitudes which inform the sage's life. Comportment and attunement are not, of course, independent. Comportment is shaped by mood, just as mood shows itself in engagement with the world.

Let's recall those little figures portrayed in landscape paintings inspired by Daoism, and their relatives who crop up in poems similarly inspired – those of Tao Qian, for instance, or Li Bai. These figures, I speculated, were epitomes of Daoist wisdom. In the sketch that follows, I try to imagine what their lives were like. What would be the tone, style, comportment and attunement of a life 'on the Way'?

In his comportment towards other people and creatures, the sage is gentle, respectful, tolerant and compassionate. For he is, after all, without a sense of himself as anything special; he does not see himself as an autonomous being set over and against other creatures which matter only as means to the satisfaction of his wants and ambitions.

In his bodily comportment, the sage is relaxed and tranquil, balanced and poised, yet possessed of vitality and energy, of a still power. He joins his body, effortlessly and easily, to the prevailing rhythms of the natural world – the seasons, patterns of weather, night and day, growth and decay. As such, he accommodates himself to the general pattern of heaven–and–earth, of a physical universe whose harmony and steadiness are preconditions for experience of a world.

What today might be called the 'lifestyle' of the sage is modest and simple, though not necessarily austere. Drinking wine or beer, enjoying conversation, listening to music played on a zither or flute – these may be among the pleasures of sages. Not among them are the pleasures that people try to obtain from self-centred and artificial desires – desires shaped by the social pressures, conventions and technological imperatives of a world divorced from natural ways of living. These are the assertive desires and pleasures of men and women who have 'lost the Way'.

What of the tone or style of the sage's conduct of everyday business, of how he goes about the world? In his actions, gestures, demeanour and speech, the sage shows himself to be responsive but steady, focused but spontaneous, firm but flexible, reserved but accessible. He follows no rigid plans, and does not espouse goals that are to be achieved come what may. Hence, he does not force people or things to fit in with plans or goals. His is not, however, the spontaneity of impulse and immediate passion: his actions are not *actes gratuits*, for this is a spontaneity that distorts reality. Instead, his is the spontaneity of a reflective person who accommodates actions and words to the way things are, not to how they seem when distorted by prejudice or passion. It is a spontaneity consonant with *dao*. The action of *dao*, too, is free from distortions and from outside pressures. *Dao*'s action, too, is never forceful, for nothing stands in its way that it needs to overcome. Its 'giving' of a world of experience is a seamless and continuous flow, and the sage's route through the world is one of unresisting and uncomplaining immersion in this flow.[7]

The sage's 'lifestyle', conduct, bodily presence and treatment of others are witness to moods and visions that make up his distinctive attunement to the world. Let me sketch in some features of this attunement.

The sage's attitude towards people's beliefs and aims, his own included, is one of irony. This is not the irony of Socrates – the pretence of accepting beliefs that one will soon debunk. Instead, it is the irony of distance. Even when the belief or aim is the sage's own, he recognises it for what it is – a component in a perspective on the world that should not pretend to objective correctness. He appreciates that there are different worlds of experience 'given' by *dao*, and that his is only one of these.

This ironic attunement to the world sits easily with the sage's 'impartiality', his reluctance to judge, discriminate or 'deem' assertively. This reticence belongs to that wider abstention from intrusive activity known as *wu wei* (see Chapter 3, page 36). He does, of course, have his preferences – finding one thing beautiful, another not; this activity worth pursuing, that one not – but he does not mistake these preferences for discoveries about an objective layout of values. And he certainly resists discriminatory treatment of creatures based on what, he knows, are fragile and revisable tastes or aversions.

The sage's irony and impartiality should not be construed as indifference or world-weariness, even if his prevailing mood is quietistic. The explanation of this mood is not indifference but, in the first place, an appreciation that people's lives go better when, in the case of conflict between their ambitions and the world, the response is not to change the world but to adjust their goals. And, second, an appreciation that the scope for anyone to change the world is narrow. The sage knows that how things fall out for him depends on the direction of a world – of the myriad things – over which he neither has, nor vainly aspires to have, control.

Ironic, impartial, quietistic – the sage may sound like a cold figure. But some further strokes to the sketch change this impression. To begin with, the sage is alert and mindful, attentive to how things themselves are. 'Things themselves', of course, are things as experienced, but there remains a difference between their presence to attentive perception and their appearance to someone too prejudiced or frenetic to register this presence. The sage's alert attentiveness is a virtue needed in order to respond appropriately to things and situations, comparable to the stillness and clarity of the water that is necessary if it is to mirror things. Still, but not rigid: for the sage's attention is not fixation on, but a flexible receptivity to, an object – a readiness to 'roam' freely in thought and imagination to wherever experience of the object might lead.

To invoke another Daoist analogy, the sage will, like a plant shoot, gradually blossom and thrive, imbued with a confidence that he is constantly growing, enriched through his interactions with creatures and things. An élan that is the antithesis of world-weariness accompanies the sage's perception of himself as an integral component – a healthy specimen – in the unfolding adventure of the "the single energy that is the world", one that is ever in the process of creation and transformation (Z 22). A comradeship that dispels indifference accompanies the sage's sense of belonging among "the ten thousand things [that] are inextricably netted together", of never being "separated off from the creatures of the world" (Z 33). The sage's wish to converge with nature reflects an appreciation of belonging within this network, of there being no dualistic divide between him and the world. The ancient sages are said, in the *Zhuangzi*, to have:

> . . . coupled heaven with earth, nourished the ten thousand things and brought the world into harmony . . . Unobstructed above, below, and all around, they connected up all that surrounded them. (Z 33)

And Zhuangzi himself – the epitome of the Daoist sage – is described as "attuning himself to whatever he encountered, thereby arriving up beyond them to the source of things" (Z 33).

Unlike the sages of some other ancient traditions, the Daoist's élan is not spoilt by a conviction that the world he experiences is an illusion, a veil behind which a truer and better reality is hidden. The world of experience does not "pass him by like an empty dream"[8] from which he is anxious to awake so as to get back to real life. For worlds of experience are the only ones there are: no structured world of things is imaginable in isolation from perspective. So the sage's world does not lose its relish or savour as a result of some vain yearning for a world beyond the veil of experience. The world of experience is as good as it gets.

But while the sage entertains no longing for a 'true world' beyond experience, he is attuned to the mystery of things – to the ineffable *dao* that is the constant well-spring and channel of experience, and hence the source of everything. The sage has, as it were, a dual vision of each being. It is at once an item defined by its place within the web of experience and something which – along with its world – is sent or given. The world of experience, for the sage, is an epiphany, the mysterious coming to presence of *dao*.

This recognition of mystery means that the sage is able, with due modesty, to see his virtues as 'profound *de*', as informed and inspired by a sense of *dao*, and as virtues therefore of a person who is 'on the Way'.

There, then, is a portrait, suggested by the classic texts, of the general comportment and attunement – the life and moods – of the Daoist sage. The task in the following chapters is to draw a more detailed picture of the Daoist's convergent relationship to natural environments and their occupants.

Mindfulness of nature

In a battered notebook, I keep a sporadic journal of encounters with wildlife and natural environments. On the eve of beginning this book, having returned from a winter walk around a bird-filled bay on the Northumberland coast, I wrote "Do I really want to write about such places or simply be in them?" The words recall the worry mentioned in the opening chapter, about whether writing about an appropriate relationship to nature is itself an appropriate way of relating to it. But

then I mentioned, too, that I wanted to put such worries aside – and that is what I have been doing.

Still, it will be good to get out into the fresh air more and to combine this with returning – after enquiring into the general philosophy of Daoism over the last two chapters – to the theme of nature.

The task is now to bring to bear upon the question of an appropriate relationship to nature the various discussions of Daoism – of, for example, its 'moods' in Chapter 2, its perception of nature as educative and edifying in Chapter 5, or the sage's virtues in Chapter 7. I'll consider these discussions in relation to issues which resonate with modern readers. Not all of the preoccupations, certainly, of 'religious' Daoism are likely to do this – not, for instance, the search for 'immortality drugs' obtained from plants, or the ambition recorded in some 'Highest Clarity School' texts[1] to embark on ecstatic journeys through the stars. But the aspects of a person's relationship to nature that I shall consider include questions such as these:

What place in this relationship do natural science and aesthetic appreciation have?

Does this relationship demand active commitment to 'saving the environment'?

Is hunting animals consistent with an appropriate relationship to them?

A Daoist perspective may not yield crisp answers to such questions, but it can guide the way in which they are addressed.

In effect, this and the following chapters develop an account of how an individual might foster convergence with the natural world. For it has been becoming clear in earlier chapters that convergence is not a single achievement – not some eureka realisation of a big truth about, say, Humanity-and-Nature. Right understanding, to be sure, is necessary for convergence. One needs, certainly, to recognise that human beings are not dualistically set apart from the natural world. But convergence itself is a complex combination of attitudes, perceptions and engagements – some of them quite simple and undramatic

– which are consonant with *dao*. A combination which is, therefore, an exercise of 'profound *de*'.

It will be useful, in the remaining chapters, to retain the rough distinction made, when discussing the Daoist sage, between 'attunement' and 'comportment' – between ways of experiencing, feeling and appreciating nature, on the one hand, and ways of acting in or towards it, on the other. It will be useful, too, to make an equally rough distinction between two broad dimensions of attunement, 'cognitive' and 'affective': between understanding, perception and contemplation, on the one hand, and moods, emotions and appreciation, on the other. In this chapter, we will look at 'cognitive' attunement to nature.

Mindfulness

'Right mindfulness' is the seventh stage on the Buddhist Eightfold Path to enlightenment, and mindfulness (*sati* in Pali) is the topic of one of the Buddha's longest and most important discourses.[2] Stripped of specifically Buddhist trappings, the term is convenient for naming the Daoist sage's cognitive stance towards the natural world. Like *sati*, this stance indicates a delicate combination of alertness, calm attention and flexible responsiveness – of the tranquillity and mental vitality applauded by Laozi (D 15). It is a combination necessary if a person is to heed Zhuangzi's injunction to "use [the] mind like a mirror" of the world (Z 7). Since no one could be 'on the Way' unless rightly attending to the world, mindfulness is a Daoist as well as a Buddhist virtue. In both traditions, it is a virtue not least because its opposite, sheer mindlessness, bears significant responsibility for people's clumsy and harmful interventions in the natural world.

Let's ask what it is to be mindful of nature. To be mindful, for example, of the little drama I recently watched on the flat roof of a house in Malta, where a large cicada and a lizard were competing for a small chunk of pear that I had dropped.

Mindfulness of this scene involves, for a start, 'disinterestedness' and impartiality. Earlier, the point was made that nature affords an opportunity for the exercise of these virtues, which may be denied in a life led predominantly among artefacts – a life of "getting and spending", to recall Wordsworth's lines, in which "the world is too much with us".[3] The present point is to recognise how the absence of these virtues compromises mindfulness.

The disinterested viewer of the roof-top drama is not without interest in it: on the contrary, it may fascinate. Such a viewer, rather, has 'un-selfed', to the degree that attention to the drama is not distorted by certain kinds of interests and predilections. Environmental writers tend to dwell on economic interests which distort people's view of the natural world, such that it is seen in terms of the profits it yields. But other interests can be equally distorting. I am not mindful of what is going on before me if I am obsessed with zoological classification of the creatures vying for the pear. ("Is it an *Egyptian* grasshopper or . . .?") Nor am I properly mindful of, say, a forest if moral outrage prevents my thinking of it as anything but the likely victim of a logging company. Un-selfing is more than the setting aside of selfish interests: it requires, too, the suspension of sentiments and concerns which, even when benign, cloud the mirror of mindful awareness.

Furthermore, I am not mindful unless I am impartial. A hatred of lizards that had me rooting for the cicada would distort my perception of the scene. G. K. Chesterton wrote that "impartiality is a pompous name for indifference", but he was wrong – about the Daoist idea of impartiality, at least. The Daoist sage, as we saw in the last chapter, is not without feelings and preferences, but, aware that these register a particular perspective that other creatures do not share, he restrains their influence on his perception and judgement. He is critical, there-fore, of people who experience animals under categories such as 'pest' or 'vermin'. Such categories do not mirror the world, for creatures that are, from one perspective, pests to be exterminated may be, from another, treasured ones deserving of special protection. (Some Sri Lankan peacocks I was admiring on a walk through a cinnamon estate were denounced as vermin by my companion – a grower of the cin-namon trees which, apparently, the birds enjoy pecking at.)

It belongs to the wider mindset of *wu wei* (non-action, or unintru-sive action) that the 'consummate person' will "sort out but not assess [or deem]" (Z 2): otherwise, he or she is failing to be mindful of the surrounding world and its creatures. This Daoist impartiality, as Guo Xiang put it, is "free from bias" and thereby "leaves all things intact" through honouring their own natures and integrity (*de*).[4] It is an impartiality attested to by the remarks in the *Zhuangzi* and the *Liezi* that mock people's mindless projection of their own aspirations and natures on to horses, birds or even trees, as we saw in Chapter 4.

Mirroring nature and 'dirty glass'

Someone is not being mindful of nature, then, when preoccupied with labelling things, nor when viewing them through the lens of categories which plainly reflect an invidious perspective. But should one go further and insist that genuinely mindful experience must dispense with concepts and words altogether? .

This issue divides nature writers. Ratchetting up his criticism of 'amateur naturalists' and bird-watchers more interested in labels than in experience (see Chapter 4, page 41), John Fowles announces, supposedly in a Zen spirit, that to apply words to a plant or animal is to insert "a pane of dirty glass between you and it". This insertion, he believes, encourages a notion of nature as "a collection of 'things' outside us".[5] In a similar vein, Annie Dillard writes that she can only "see truly" when she silences all "verbalization" and "interior babble". Once she classifies or describes what is before her, she continues, she "cease[s] to see the mountain or feel the puppy". Like Fowles's dirty glass, she has become "opaque", like "asphalt".[6]

By contrast, Richard Mabey rejects these images of language as an "impassable barrier between us and nature". Indeed, when used imaginatively, language "resonates, chimes sympathetically with nature" and is a means for "re-engaging with it".[7]

Where does the Daoist stand on this issue? A case might be assembled for thinking that Daoism is on the side of Fowles and Dillard. There are chapters in the *Daodejing* that disparage the use of words and unfavourably contrast intellectual learning with genuine knowledge. "Those who talk do not know" (D 56) and "Those who know are not full of knowledge" (D 81). Then there are passages that envisage and extol an experience of things which transcends any conceptual understanding of them. The most important of these, perhaps, are Zhuangzi's remarks on "the fasting of the mind", which is said to "expel" (intellectual) knowledge (*zhi*) and bring about an "emptiness" of mind, a state "beyond the mind's understanding consciousness". The person who is fasting perceives things with "the vital energy (*qi*) rather than with the mind", and is able thereby to "await the presence of beings" in stillness (Z 4).

Interpretation of these passages is a delicate matter, and the texts are not entirely consistent on this difficult topic. In my judgement, however, we shouldn't understand the passages as saying that things are truly encountered only in experiences 'purified' of conceptual understanding. The *Daodejing's* animosity to 'those who talk' and are 'full of knowledge' is specifically towards people who pretend they can articulate what *dao* is like. *Dao*, I have argued, is not ineffable because it is a very peculiar object, but because it is not an object at all, since it is the source of all objects. The ineffability of *dao*, then, does nothing to support the suggestion that authentic experience of such objects as mountains, puppies or plants must be cleansed of concepts under which they are experienced.

It's hard to see, too, how a yearning for 'pure' experience could be reconciled with perspectivism. For Daoists, an object does not exist independently of the perspectives – the ways of perception and conceptualisation – through which they are experienced. To insist that we should see something as it is, without the 'dirty glass' of concepts intervening, is to imagine that it could be viewed not as a mountain, not as a puppy, not as this or that, not as any particular thing. For to view it as something is to do so from a perspective, a point of view. No sense can be made of an object – an 'it' – lurking behind perspectives which, like so many veils, might be torn away so as to reveal the object in its naked truth.

That said, the Daoist has great sympathy with the complaints that inspire a yearning for 'pure' experience. Fowles is right to lament the hegemony of a dissective, analytical attitude towards the natural world, just as Dillard is to regret people's 'opacity' to creatures and environments. Indeed, it is precisely as making such complaints that Zhuangzi's call for a 'fasting of the mind' should be read. The 'emptiness' or suspension of 'understanding consciousness' commended, however, is not that of a mind which, no longer deflected by concepts, homes in on objects like a laser beam. Rather it is the 'stilled' state of someone receptive to experience, who 'waits for the presence of beings' and intuitively responds to them. It is the 'unscurrying' state of a person whose experience is not occluded by preoccupations with self, nor with labelling and analysing.

Zhuangzi also sympathises with the complaint that words can distort experience. This is not, though, because language as such is a distorting lens or dirty glass, but because people mistake the status of language, wrongly imagining that it can and should capture things as they objectively are. This encourages an obsession with naming things, a rigidity in the use of words, and a hostility to imaginative, metaphorical speech. A truer view of language – of names and descriptions as necessarily registering perspectives – encourages a freer, more flexible, more poetic relationship to speech. Invoking a characteristically aquatic image, derived from a goblet designed to tip and then right itself when overfull, Zhuangzi commends what he calls "spillover saying" (Z 27). As one commentator explains, this is "speech characterised by the intelligent spontaneity of Daoist behaviour in general, a fluid language which keeps its equilibrium through changing meanings and viewpoints".[8]

The task, then, when in the presence of nature, is not to suppress the words ordinarily applied to creatures and phenomena. To register the lizard as a lizard, the cicada as a cicada, is fine. The task, rather, is to remain pliant and responsive in how one goes on to describe them – to be open, say, to metaphors which speak imaginatively about the little battle over a chunk of pear. When used like this, speech may indeed, as Mabey put it, resonate with the natural world, for it then reflects the fluidity and transformations in our experience of natural things. Speech which chimes in this way is part of, not an obstacle to, mindful attunement to nature.

Science and reverie

Daoism, then, rejects the idea of mindfulness as 'pure', concept-free experience of nature. It also rejects, but with less sympathy, the proposal that mindfulness is the prerogative of scientific enquiry. The idea that, to be properly cognisant of nature, one must defer to the natural sciences is, of course, a familiar one in our own times – pervasive, for example, in environmental education and in 'nature programmes' on television.

Daoism's rejection of this view is not due to hostility towards science. Both the *Daodejing* and the *Zhuangzi* subscribe to the cosmology of their age, to the doctrine that the myriad things are formed through vital energies (*qi*) derived from the operation of *yin* and *yang* (D 42, Z 17). Later Daoist-inspired texts incorporate the theory of the 'Five Processes (or 'Doings')' and their 'correlatives' (see Chapter 5, page 51), and later still, in 'religious' texts such as the fourth-century-CE *Baopuzi*,[9] the study of minerals such as gold and cinnabar is deemed essential to the search for an elixir which will guarantee 'ascension' to eternal heavenly existence.

Nor did Daoists deny that cosmological understanding could confirm, even heighten, awareness of a person's place in the scheme of things. I'm less likely to "make too much of myself" for example, when I learn that the energy coursing through me also courses through everything (Z 17). In the *Huainanzi* especially, reflection on *qi* and *yin* and *yang*, on the Five Processes and related phenomena, is held to encourage a tranquil, even joyful sense of one's integral place in the 'great merging' of all things.[10]

It is one thing, however, to endorse the scientific wisdom of one's times and to grant it a potentially salutary role, but quite another thing to insist that someone is mindful of the natural world only, or primarily, when submitting it to the scientific gaze. For the Daoist, there is nothing privileged about a scientific account of the world. Granted, good scientists will set aside various human interests and feelings that might cloud their enquiries, but the accounts they arrive at are no less perspectival than any others. The scientist describes the world from certain angles of interest – in the prediction and control of events, in taking things apart and making them, in finding cause-and-effect explanations, and so on. The concepts science deploys – from *qi* to gravity, from the Five Processes to genes – are shaped by such interests just as surely as the concepts used by art critics are shaped by very different concerns.

Nor, for the Daoist, does the scientist's way of observing the world of nature have any primacy. My notebook entry for 2 October 2009, recalling a walk on the harbour wall of a fishing village in Fife, reads:

A vivid moment – a large fulmar flying a few feet from my face, very slowly. Acute sense of its weight and density – and its cold back eyes looking into mine. Strong sense, too, of the bird's close connection to everything around – fishing nets, the seaweed on the harbour wall, men scrubbing down boats, threatening clouds, distant screeches.

This records, I think, a mindful moment: no less mindful than one that a professional ornithologist, exercising specialist expertise, might have. It's certainly not the case that an ornithological description tells the truth about the fulmar whereas my little entry does not.

The claim that only the scientist's attention is properly mindful of nature implies that authentic experience of nature is confined to people with specialist theoretical knowledge. This is an implication which Daoists reject. Recall their admiration for the implicit 'know-how' of the fishermen, craftsmen and other figures said to be 'on the Way'. Mindfulness is something that men and women without scientific expertise may possess. And, one should add, that people *with* this expertise may also possess. Being a professional scientist does not preclude the mindfulness which Daoists encourage, but this is a mindfulness exercised 'off duty', as it were, and is not to be equated with scientific attention to the world.

Anstruther, a fishing village in Fife.

Indeed, for Laozi and Zhuangzi, a professional scientific stance towards nature might obstruct mindfulness. For it is a stance which is too dogged, too much dictated by a ground plan, too rigidly focused on the achievement of goals – overturning a hypothesis about bird behaviour, discovering a new species of reptile, identifying a plant's medical potential, finding the cause of a tree blight, or whatever. The *Huainanzi* remarks that "those who have investigated things ultimately rest with non-action (*wu wei*)". Whether or not there was a truth to this remark in the context of second-century-BCE Chinese cosmological enquiry, it could not be plausibly maintained that *wu wei* – the relaxed spontaneity advocated by Daoism – is a feature of modern scientific practice.

If mindful experience of nature is neither 'pure' and concept-free nor confined to experts, how, in a word, might it be characterised – a word that would gather together the aspects of mindfulness which have been emerging over the last few pages? Shortly, I'll propose such a word, but first a few remarks on a theme in the *Zhuangzi* which inspires the proposal.

This is the theme of *yu*, variously rendered as roaming, rambling, wandering. We briefly encountered it earlier, when citing a famous reference to poets whose eyes and hearts-and-minds ramble among the 'manifold riches of the earth' (see Chapter 5, page 55). As the reference indicates, roaming is a metaphor, drawn from a loose and easy style of exploring nature, for a way of experiencing things. The sage, it is said, is a roamer: hence, like a free-spirited backpacker – the *Wanderer* celebrated in German *Lieder* – he is unconcerned with profit, destinations, goals, obligations or commitments, and eschews analytical enquiry which "chops things into pieces" (Z 5).

The metaphor is elaborated in Guo Xiang's commentary on a passage from Chapter 1 of the *Zhuangzi* ('Roaming without a destination') which refers to the wandering of the sage's heart-and-mind. The sage is implicitly compared to the leisurely rambler who allows himself to be guided by shifting terrains and glimpses of new vistas, who becomes absorbed in the landscape, and – without a fixed destination – enjoys a sense of freedom in the environment through which he journeys. The sage's mind, analogously, "wanders in the paths of transformation", "follows along with the character of each thing", is expansive and "unfettered", "free of dependence . . . unobstructed", and is delivered from an opposition of "self and other" which occludes an attentive openness to things.[11]

We'll see in a later chapter that roaming is not merely a metaphor, for rambling in landscapes is itself edifying. It at once represents and nurtures mindful experience. That's why the wandering of the sage's heart-and-mind is enhanced by "being in a vast mountain forest" (Z 26).

Partly inspired by the theme of roaming in the *Zhuangzi*, here is the word I propose for characterising mindfulness: *reverie*. A more immediate inspiration is a much later work whose very title relates rambling to an attunement to nature – Jean-Jacques Rousseau's *Reveries of a Solitary Walker*. A still more recent inspiration is the writing, such as *The Poetics of Reverie*, of Rousseau's twentieth-century admirer, the French scientist and philosopher Gaston Bachelard.

'Reverie' will sound a strange choice if we think of it as idle, semi-comatose day-dreaming, but that is not what Rousseau and Bachelard intend by the term, even if they invest it with certain features associated with day-dreaming – tranquillity, divorce from the business of life, surrender to the imagination. For both writers, crucially, reverie is a form of attentiveness, of 'alert consciousness' – specifically an openness to the presence and 'reverberations' of things, a welcoming in of what Bachelard calls 'the space of elsewhere'.[12] As such, reverie is a 'disinterested' state, a way of 'contemplating' plants and other natural beings in which, Rousseau writes, our "passions and practical concerns"[13] are in abeyance.

Reverie is contrasted not only with pragmatic attention to nature but also with more regimented forms of reflection – with deliberation and analysis:

> Reverie relaxes and amuses me; reflection tires and saddens me; thinking was always painful and charmless for me … During [reveries] my soul rambles and glides through the universe on the wings of imagination.[14]

Reverie, says Rousseau, is spontaneous and 'entirely free' attention in which ideas "follow their own bent without [the] constraint" and direction imposed in furrow-browed deliberation or analysis.[15] Being free and spontaneous, Bachelard remarks – in words that evoke Daoism's favourite metaphor – reverie imparts "a feeling of flowing onward". Indeed, such is this feeling of participation in an ever-transforming world of experience that the 'I' engaged in reverie "no longer opposes itself to the world".[16] His words recall Rousseau's observation that reverie allows him to "forget himself" and to feel "one" with the "beautiful system" of nature, to experience "the spectacle of nature . . . in its wholeness".[17]

The holistic, convergent tenor of these remarks is dramatised in Bachelard's reference to reverie as giving us "the whole of the whole . . . a unity of [a] world" which is compared to a single "gigantic fruit".[18] This image is, perhaps, misleading: for what provides a sense of unity and convergence is not a vision of reality as a single object which, for convenience, we slice into separate segments. Rather, it is the ease and inevitability with which, in reverie, the mind passes from one thing to another, makes this or that association, 'flows onward' to a new image or thought.

The world of experience in which reverie freely moves is a limit-less web from which nothing is left out, including those beings – our-selves – who attend to it. Almost anything may prompt and guide a particular route through this web: half-remembered lines of poetry, a recently read book on botany, recollections of some episode in one's life, images of people and animals who have mattered to one, a sense of a place's beauty, a philosophical thought, an insistent tune in one's head. For example, Bachelard describes a reverie which starts with attention to a bird's nest. This reverie has no cut-off point or terminus. Looking at this "precarious" nest leads to thoughts of other fragile objects, then to images of security (of home and household), then to the idea of the well-being of one's own and other people's children, then to larger speculations on confidence in the regular workings of nature, then to . . .[19]

The same goes for my little reverie as I watched the lizard and cicada warring over the pear. Attention to the lizard refers me to the ancient wall it must have climbed up, and from there to the elements – rain, wind, sun – that gave the wall its look. These in turn refer me to the nearby megalithic temples that are now being protected against the elements, and the temples refer me to the people who once sought protection inside the temples. The thought of those people in turn refers me to the creatures they would have lived alongside — to the distant ancestors of the cicada a few feet away from my chair, or to . . .

The idea of reverie gathers together the aspects of mindfulness which emerged earlier in this chapter. Reverie is the grain of mind, the orientation, of someone, like the Daoist sage, who is mindful of nature. In reverie, a person sees things as they are. Not through penetrating a veil of appearance to a world free from all perspective, for there is no such world. Reverie, rather, is alertness — undistorted by prejudice, passion and purpose — to the places occupied by beings in the great open web of the world of experience. It is a gentle reverie when Tao Qian, in his poem 'Returning to live in the country (I)', having observed how:

> The caged bird wants the old trees and air.
> Fish in their pool miss the ancient stream.

is brought to reflect on how he too has been:

> Too long a prisoner, captive in a cage,
> Now I can get back to Nature.[20]

Bachelard makes a large claim on behalf of reverie: "the values that mark reverie", he writes, "mark humanity in its depths".[21] But the claim is no larger than the one Buddhists make on behalf of mindfulness as the principal virtue of a human being's cognitive relationship to the world.[22] It is a claim, too, in a recognisably Daoist key.

Nature, feeling and appreciation

A Daoist attunement to the natural world, then, is one of mindfulness or reverie. More precisely – to recall a distinction I made in the last chapter – this is its 'cognitive' attunement. I now turn to more 'affective' modes of attunement: to feelings, moods and enjoyment. I begin by identifying a primary or 'default' mode of feeling for nature suggested by Daoist texts.

Sober joy

Despite Daoism's reputation among New Agers as spiritual ecology, the classic texts are devoid of dithyrambic odes to nature. They contain none of the rhetoric of 'awe and wonder' at nature which fill the pages of Thoreau, John Muir or Rachel Carson. Nevertheless, the overarching mood or feeling towards nature which Daoism encourages is a positive one. I'll call it 'sober joy'.

Sobriety is to be expected, given that the virtues of the Daoist sage include restraint, equanimity and moderation. He is "cautious", "reserved" and eschews experiences that might "unhinge the mind" or "disrupt the senses" (D 12, 15) – not at all the nature-intoxicated figure of Romantic literature and art.

The poetry that Daoism inspired indicates, moreover, that pleasure is experienced less in the dramatic and showier marvels of nature than in the small and ordinary. It is in chrysanthemums, small birds and mountain air that Tao Qian finds enjoyment, and he wonders what pleasures can compare to the feel of "light rain [and] a breeze".[1]

'Tao Qian Enjoying Chrysanthemums', Du Jin.
© Metropolitan Museum of Art / Art Resource / Scala, Florence

Gnarled trees, circling fish, reeds on a river bank – these are among the natural phenomena that give quiet delight to the Tang poets. Meng Haoran, for example, is moved to play his zither and find someone to share his pleasure with when, through the open window:

A breeze brings in the fragrance of the lotus [and]
Night-time dew on bamboo drips with a clear sound.[2]

This sober joy in the unremarkable is something that several contemporary nature writers also experience. One of them is "enchanted" by watching two ants meeting, by cow parsley and a green shield beetle. For him, as for the Daoist, impartiality in the presence of nature requires mindfulness and openness to the humble and inconspicuous, as well as to the awesome. A patch of grass, to the mindful observer, is "a jungle in miniature".[3]

People's pleasure in nature should also be sober if they are mindful of the ephemerality – the 'rising and falling' – of everything in nature. Melancholic sensitivity among the Chinese to the passing of things may not have been as acute as in refined circles of Heian Japan, but it is nevertheless invoked by Daoist writers. The joy and happiness that mountain forests and great plains would otherwise inspire in him are, Zhuangzi says, tempered by sorrow at the temporary character of life (Z 22).

But is it right to consider that joy is the default mood towards nature that Daoism endorses? There are, after all, passages where Daoist thinkers appear to criticise this feeling. Guo Xiang, for instance, observes that there is no place for joy or sorrow once it is accepted that everything necessarily follows the course of nature. But the joy for which he finds no place is not, I think, the sober joy of which I am speaking, but a wilder and more swooning emotion. And certainly there are invitations in Daoist writings to experience the mood I have in mind.

In the works of philosophers and poets alike, there is recognition of the importance of contentment (zu) in a life that is 'on the Way' (D 44, 46). This is a tranquil contentment which, as Tao Qian knew, could not be achieved in 'the dust-filled trap' of a busy, febrile city. Contented people need quiet and space, which is one reason why "being in a vast mountain forest benefits a man" (Z 26). This is not, however, the contentment of a lotus-eater or couch potato, for it is infused with an élan which converts it into joy.

In the *Zhuangzi*, different aspects of a joy infused with élan are described. In a remarkable passage from Chapter 14, the élan is a vivid sense, in the presence of nature, of spontaneity. Here, the legendary Yellow Emperor both speaks of and exemplifies this joyful spontaneity when he plays music in the wilderness of Dongting. "I played", he says, with "tireless sounds, adjusting to the unforced mandates of things . . . the music sprang into motion from no specifiable place". "Moving, flowing, unforced and uncontrived", it was a "heavenly music" and a "heavenly joy". (Interestingly, the Chinese term for music, '*yue*', was originally the same as the term for joy.) In this connection, one thinks too of Zhuangzi's happy swimmers – human and piscine – who delight in free, unforced movements that do not impose on their environment.

In the Yellow Emperor passage another aspect of joy is alluded to. Spontaneous, responsive music is compared to the understanding of the sage who does not impose himself on things, and thereby honours "their own mandates". Indeed, he "takes joy in clearing the way for things", enabling them to figure in experience as what they themselves are (Z 6). There is an élan in seeing oneself as providing the myriad things with a space in which they are 'let be', so that they may be authentically present to our experience.

Finally, there is the quiet yet energising joy of appreciating that, notwithstanding their individual integrity, all natural beings are united as 'gifts' of a single source, *dao*. Joy accompanies the breakthrough of the sage to "a comprehensive view of everything as one" (Z 25), just as it accompanies the understanding of, say, a swimmer or carpenter, that it is the Way of something – water or wood – that he or she is following.

This indicates that Daoist mindfulness involves, in effect, a dual vision of each being in its individual integrity *and* in its belonging to *dao* (see page 80). Mindfulness, it emerges, is not a merely cognitive attunement to the natural world, for it also embraces a mood – the sober joy inspired by experiencing the world as one that is given by *dao*.

Opposing moods

Here are some lines from a novel by the Austrian novelist Thomas Bernhard:

> I do not know nature at all and I hate it . . . I love everything except nature, because nature seems to me uncanny and I have experienced its malignancy and ruthlessness . . . I fear it and avoid it wherever I can . . . the countryside is always against me.[4]

Expressed here are feelings too dark to qualify even as *sober* joy in the presence of nature. Bernhard experiences nature as alien and uncanny, indifferent or malignant towards him, ruthless and cruel. Nature should be hated, feared and avoided – not celebrated.

Is there something wrong with Bernhard – and with others who, in Woody Allen's phrase, feel resolutely 'at two with nature'? Or something wrong with you and me, for ignoring or condoning aspects of the natural world which legitimately invite fear and horror? And, how might Daoists respond to Bernhard's diatribe?

Regarding the suggestion that people should shun nature because of the indifference towards them of wild animals and other living beings, we can be brief. It is no part of the case for sober joy that nature should reciprocate and care about us. Babies are indifferent to the attentions of most adults, but this doesn't destroy the pleasure people enjoy in the company of infants. For me to be affected by the indifference of the birds I feed each morning would betray a self-centredness which Daoists – and not just they – rightly denounce.

We can be brief, too, with the point about nature's sometimes uncanny and alien otherness. This was discussed in Chapter 4, where it became clear that the convergence Daoists seek with the natural world is consistent with a sense of the otherness of, say, the fishes and birds described by Zhuangzi. The case for convergence appeals not to alleged similarities between humans and other living beings, but – as explained in Chapter 6 – to the intimate co-dependence of beings, us included. To recall Zhuangzi's words, *dao* "opens [things] into one another, connecting them to form a oneness" (Z 2). I don't have to think I am much like the birds I feed to realise that, at a deep level, neither they nor I could exist in isolation from one another, that they and I do not occupy independent spheres of being.

It is possible, in any case, to exaggerate the uncanniness of other creatures. Often they are no harder to understand than human beings whose tastes, beliefs and ambitions are very different from our own. The initially strange behaviour − jumping up, flying a few metres, landing − of some crows I am watching on a Sri Lankan beach soon becomes clear: they are *teasing* the dogs that are trying to catch them. The sympathetic remarks of Zhuangzi and Liezi on animals − their natures, pleasures and sufferings − indicate that for these Daoists nature is not an unfathomable, uncanny realm in the presence of which one can only feel a sense of utter separation.

Even if the world of nature, in some of its manifestations, is emphatically other, why should this preclude a feeling of joy? Experience of the 'sheer alien pointless independent existence' of wild creatures, as Iris Murdoch called it, might be just what is needed to prise a person from self-centred absorption in the all-too-worldly business that obstructs spontaneous enjoyment. Many nature writers, certainly, attest to the need they feel to regard wild creatures − or indeed their own pet cats − now as 'friends' and now as "expressions of compelling otherness in nature";[5] "now as 'familiar' and now as 'strange'".[6] For these writers, experience of a creature's otherness does not threaten Zhuangzi's feeling for what "ties all things together" (Z 6).

But what of nature's 'malignancy and ruthlessness', the main cause of Bernhard's fear and hatred? My sporadic journal records encounters with suffering − a lamb with eyes pecked out by crows, a rabbit screaming as a weasel drags it over a wall, a bee buzzing hysterically as a spider slowly eats it. Readers will have had their own encounters and watched TV wildlife documentaries which, for some of them, confirm an impression of nature as a "scene of horror",[7] a "repulsive cesspit" that "deserves to be wiped out in a holocaust".[8] Interestingly, however, some testimonies to harshness and suffering in nature come not from those who hate and want to 'wipe out' nature, but from writers who express a love of nature and an aspiration for convergence with it. The gruesome, violent aspects of natural life on which, for example,

Thoreau and the American poet Robinson Jeffers dwell are, for them, no reason to adopt a default attitude of fear, horror or hatred.

These aspects were not ignored in the Daoist classics, where there are references to the dangers posed by sharks, tigers and dragons. The response of the travelling sage to these dangers is not derring-do or "the bravery of the hunter", but the quiet courage of someone who is "perspicuous about safety and danger", careful and calm (Z 17; see D 73). The texts do not directly address the question of whether awareness of ubiquitous suffering in the natural world should diminish, or even annul, sober joy. But it is not difficult to guess how Daoist thinkers might reply to Bernhard and other haters of nature.

They would point out, first, that mindful attention to the natural world would challenge the bleak portrayal of it on which the haters rely. Ordinary observation combines with professional studies of animals to demonstrate that "contrary to the popular myth, life in the wild is not relentlessly harsh; survival and pleasure are mutually compatible".[9] Indeed, pleasure is adaptive, for to enjoy doing – and doing well – what contributes to survival enhances the prospects for survival. Granted, many birds die young and often painfully, but no honest observer could deny the pleasure that millions of birds take in flying, singing, mating and bathing. One may draw attention, as Buddhists and biologists both like to do, to the thousands of animals suffering and dying during the typing of a single sentence – but one should also mention the billions of creatures who are enjoying themselves during this same period. Zhuangzi and Liezi are as alert to the pleasures experienced by fish, birds and horses – when these are left to live naturally – as to death and pain in the wild.

Another characteristically Daoist response to the haters of nature will be rejection of the whole vocabulary – 'malignancy', 'viciousness', 'ruthlessness', 'wastefulness', 'repulsiveness', 'cruelty' – deployed to induce a negative view of it. This vocabulary, like that of 'vermin' and 'pests', betrays a partiality and invidious 'deeming' which the mindful Daoist sage rises above. While we are nowadays alert to the inappropriateness of rose-tinted depictions of 'cute' animals, we are less alert to the distortions of negative, but equally anthropomorphic, descriptions of other animals. This is not to deny that an individual animal may act viciously, inflicting gratuitous pain on its victim. But it is silly to categorise the daily killing of prey by predators, of flies by flycatchers, of little fish by big ones, as vicious, cruel or ruthless. Silly, as well, to compare the mortality rate among fledglings or tadpoles, say, with the wastefulness characteristic of modern consumer societies.

The lexicon of 'malignancy', 'ruthlessness', 'wastefulness' and the rest gets its sense in the context of human behaviour. Genocide is ruthless; profligate spending is wasteful; sadistic torture is malign. In particular and perhaps rare cases, an animal's behaviour may be sufficiently analogous to human action for such terms to be applicable to it, but the terms lose their bite, their sense even, when indiscriminately applied to the normal, natural behaviour of a species.

The Daoist would explain, finally, that to experience sober joy is not to *endorse* the natural world. This feeling is independent of judgements concerning the intrinsic value of nature or a balance of good over evil in the animal realm. Joy is not a judgement or evaluation, not something that statistics of death and suffering might contradict. Indeed, the very idea of a value intrinsic in nature is incoherent for a Daoist, since judgements of value, like all judgements, inevitably register a particular perspective. Equally, there can be no objective calculation of the good and evil present in the natural world, for this would be, impossibly, a calculation made from nowhere, from no point of view – not mine, yours, a dog's, a fish's, a grasshopper's, a tree's, not anything's. The mindful and impartial sage recognises this: that's why he refrains from 'deeming' and, in this as in other respects, adheres to *wu wei*.

Enjoying natural beauty

Just as readers have been disturbed by spectacles of suffering in nature, so they have been moved by ones of natural beauty. Only an hour ago, I was sitting in a small arbour of my garden, surrounded by roses and foxgloves, dewy grass beneath my bare feet, watching a pair of spotted flycatchers coaxing their young into taking their first flight. Who would deny that this is an experience of beauty and that such experiences are an important component of many people's enjoyment of the natural world?

It can come as a surprise, therefore, to learn that ecologists and environmental ethicists are often critical of people for whom aesthetic appreciation is a significant aspect of their admiration for nature. A further surprise is the sheer number of objections that have been made to an aesthetic stance towards natural environments. The charge is made, for instance, that appreciation of beauty is too volatile and idiosyncratic to be a reliable, stable guide to environmental policy. Or that, in comparison with the knowledge provided by biologists and zoologists, aesthetic enjoyment is too superficial, too lightweight to be a basis for serious respect for plant life and wild animals.[10]

On these criticisms, the Daoist spends little time. The Daoist focus is on an individual's relationship to nature, not on environmental policy: so, even if aesthetic enjoyment makes no contribution to policy, this is not a reason to impugn it. Nor, as we saw in the last chapter, does the Daoist privilege scientific understanding over other forms of experience. Openness to beauty may be as mindful a way of experiencing nature as that of the botanist.

But there are further criticisms of the aesthetic stance which the Daoist takes more seriously. One such criticism is that this stance fails to respect the integrity of natural beings. The aesthetic attitude to things is an anthropocentric one, encouraging appreciation of things solely according to the pleasurable experiences they provide for human beings. It is an essentially exploitative attitude: the aesthete mines the world for what it can yield – not raw materials, as in the case of the engineer, but sensations and thrills.

A related complaint is that enjoyment of beauty is judgemental and discriminatory: for to regard a place or a creature as beautiful is to contrast it with ones that are not. This discrimination is not harmless, since the invidious distinctions people make impact badly on creatures and places deemed ugly or unattractive. We protect butterflies, but squash cockroaches; conserve a grove of oaks, but build a car park on the nearby scrubland. These criticisms deserve consideration, since Daoist virtues, we know, include respect for the integrity of things and impartiality. But, first, we should look at what is said about beauty in the Daoist texts.

Actually, it's not a simple matter to identify what is said. This is because – as in ancient Greek – terms translatable as 'beautiful' and 'ugly' can also, in context, be translated as 'good' and 'bad'. Where one translator of the *Daodejing* renders '*mei*', for example, as 'beautiful', another may render it as 'fair', 'fine' or simply 'good'.[11] This is emphatically *not* because the Chinese terms are ambiguous, with both an aesthetic and an ethical sense. Rather, as we shall see, it is because Daoist thinkers – like their Greek contemporaries – recognised an intimate relationship between what we moderns have come to separate out as beauty and the good.

Despite this difficulty, we may identify some characteristic Daoist thoughts on beauty. To begin with, the beauty we find in things is typically perspectival. Actual or possible differences in what people, and other creatures, find beautiful – lepers or courtesans, fish or women (Z 2) – are among Zhuangzi's favourite examples for illustrating his claim that the qualities we discern do not belong to a reality independent of experience. Second, beauty and ugliness, as ordinarily experienced, are correlative: when people "know the beautiful as beauty, there arises the recognition of the ugly" (D 2). Finding the butterfly beautiful, it seems, means finding some other creatures, like cockroaches, repulsive.

It looks, then, as if the Daoist will endorse the complaints that aesthetic appreciation of natural things is anthropocentric and discriminatory. In calling butterflies beautiful, it appears, we speak from a standpoint not shared by other creatures or even by human beings in other times or climes. And we do so in a manner that discriminates between butterflies and other living beings, with unfortunate results for the latter.

The matter is, however, more nuanced. This is because Daoist philosophers, again like the Greeks, distinguish between different kinds or concepts of beauty: one which does not, and others which do, have an important role in our relationship to nature.

On the one hand is the beauty we experience, in everyday life, when we find that this or that sight, smell or sound gives pleasure. It is this beauty – beauty as the source of pleasant feelings – which, for environmentalist critics and Daoists alike, is anthropocentric and discriminatory. It is beauty which, if granted too large a place in our concerns, is destructive of an appropriate attunement to the natural world, for it belongs with the view of nature as a resource for the production of human satisfactions. Zhuangzi and Guo Xiang both issue warnings against taking judgements of beauty in this sense too seriously, as if they were *more* than particular perspectival responses.

But the Daoist allows for other notions of beauty, ones largely ignored since the emergence of modern aesthetics in eighteenth-century Europe with its myopic concentration on beauty as a source of sensations. Appreciation of these other modes of beauty is, for the Daoist, integral to an appropriate relationship to nature. It is an appreciation inseparable from the mindful *de* of the sage.

In his 1844 essay 'Nature', Ralph Waldo Emerson wrote:

> There is nothing so wonderful in any particular landscape as the necessity of being beautiful under which every landscape lies. Nature cannot be surprised in her undress. Beauty breaks in everywhere.[12]

This is not the beauty that a butterfly has and a cockroach lacks, but a beauty belonging to the world as a whole. For Emerson, this is because nature is a 'symbol of spirit' that courses through the world.

A comparable thought is found in Daoist texts. Zhuangzi points out that, while lots of people "try to judge the [many] beauties of heaven and earth", only a few appreciate the single "beauty of heaven and earth" as a whole. These few are people whom *dao* "allows to be inwardly sage", and who therefore recognise the world they experience as a gift of *dao* (Z 33; see Z 22). Guo Xiang similarly contrasts the beauties available to people who judge from their individual standpoints with the beauty accessible to someone who "takes the vast, all-pervading view of things". For Daoists, the world takes on the aspect of beauty – it becomes a world to savour and delight in – when it is seen for what it is, an experiential whole whose source is *dao*. Delight in particular things – a bird's plumage, say, or the sound of a waterfall – is in turn deepened when they are experienced as integrated in this whole.

It goes without saying that this delight is not heated and histrionic, but a restrained, steady, unforced and peaceful delight suited to the sage and his virtues. And mention of these virtues points to a further mode of beauty whose appreciation is integral to a Daoist relationship to nature.

Remember that some Chinese terms may be rendered in English by both aesthetic and ethical adjectives – by 'beautiful' and 'good'. This indicates a perception in Chinese philosophy of an intimate connection between beauty and goodness or virtue. It is a connection which has been largely lost in modern Western thought, where the tendency has been sharply to contrast, even to oppose, aesthetic and moral values. This is a loss one should regret, for it is impossible fully to understand the sense of beauty without recognising its relationship to the good. Specifically, there is a kind of beauty we appreciate in nature precisely when creatures, places or processes are experienced as symbols of virtue. Experienced, more exactly, as having those qualities – such as grace, restraint and spontaneity – which in the case of a human being are virtues.[13]

For the Daoist, as for the Greeks and for Buddhists, beauty of this kind is, in the first instance, beauty of the person, which manifests itself in the demeanour and comportment of the virtuous person. As Zhuangzi observes, the person who has achieved understanding, harmony and bodily discipline is one whom virtue, *de*, has "made beautiful" (Z 22). In nature, we experience beauty where we find symbols of, or analogies with, this beauty of the virtuous person.

It is no accident that the natural beauty celebrated in Chinese poetry and painting is the beauty of things that are epiphanies of, or metaphors for, the virtues. The famous bamboo paintings of the fourteenth-century artist Ni Zan (Ni Tsan) depict trees which – pliant, straight, hollow – had become conventional symbols for the flexibility, uprightness and humble receptiveness of the sage. Ni Zan's own life, in fact, was something of a symbol for these sagely virtues. During the upheavals of the Mongol occupation of China, he gave up his considerable wealth and property in order to wander freely and unencumbered through the landscapes that he so memorably recorded.

Unsurprisingly, given the 'root' metaphor of water, it is in depictions of water that artists and poets attest most clearly to the intimacy of beauty and virtue. The still, "limpid waters mirroring the reeds" provide Wang Wei with a metaphor for the "quiet, clear and tranquil" mind of the person beautified by *de*.[14] The lively waterfall that a sage admires, in paintings like Ma Yuan's, is a favoured Daoist symbol of the free-flowing spontaneity achieved by the sage.

A sense of the beauty of the *dao*-given world as a whole and enjoyment of natural beauty as an analogy or mirror of the virtues – both forms of appreciation take their place alongside, or indeed blend into, the sober joy of people attuned to nature in a Daoist key.

'A Branch of Bamboo', Ni Zan.
© Freer Gallery of Art, Smithsonian Institution, Washington, D.C.

Engaging with nature

We've gained an idea, over the last two chapters, of Daoist attunement to the natural world – of mindful, soberly joyful and appreciative experience of this world. But how might a suitably attuned person *act*, both in and towards natural environments? What does he or she *do* by way of engaging with and intervening in nature? These are questions to address as attention now turns from attunement to comportment.

Activity, engagement, intervention

Someone might suggest that these questions have, for a Daoist, a quick answer. The sage will *do* little or nothing. Otherwise he would be unfaithful to the spirit of 'stillness' and *wu wei* ('non-action') that permeates the virtuous Daoist life. Laozi, after all, tells us that the sage "knows without going about . . . and accomplishes through non-action" (D 47).

But this proposal would be mistaken. We know, for a start, that *wu wei* is not a static, purely contemplative condition. If it were, the call to "be active, but have no activities" (D 63) would be unintelligible, as would Zhuangzi's remark that "activity . . . cannot be avoided" (Z 19). *Wu wei* is spontaneous action which responds to how things are. It is not *doing* things as such that is unfaithful to *wu wei*, but doing them according to a rigid plan and in pursuit of fixed goals.

It would be hard, too, to reconcile opposition to action with the admiration expressed in the classic texts for skilled practical people – craftsmen, cicada catchers, farmers, boatmen – whose knowledge is, as it were, 'in the hands'. Indeed, we noted that there is a primacy to this practical know-how, and the knowledge of the immobile spectator or the supine scholar is secondary.

It is true that Daoists commend the stillness or tranquillity of the person attuned to nature, but this is not a stillness that excludes action and being up and about. On the contrary, there are passages where, drawing on the metaphor of water, the point is made that genuine stillness requires movement. In words that Martin Heidegger had inscribed on a scroll hanging in his study, the *Daodejing* compares the tranquillity of the sage to the stillness which water needs if the mud is to clear, but adds that the same sage, through his vital activity, "makes the still gradually come to life" (D 15). As Zhuangzi explains, disturbed water is cloudy, but is also so when "clogged and dammed". If "it does not flow it can never be clear". Stillness and motion – whether of water or the sage – complement each other in a pairing of "the power in *yin*" and "the surge of *yang*" (Z 15).

Finally, it is evident from the literature that Daoists do not just sit and stare, but actively participate in the outdoor life. Zhuangzi himself is described as walking in the mountains, fishing, and strolling along river banks and over bridges. The poet Li Bai "loved to go roaming on celebrated mountains",[1] and in later centuries Daoist temples in the mountains became favourite sites for excursions into nature.

Special mention should be made of the practice, among people of Confucian and Daoist sensibilities alike, of composing or performing poetry and music in natural environments. The poems composed near the Orchid Pavilion, to which the calligrapher Wang Xizhi wrote his famous preface, were nothing unusual (see page 55). As for music, it was not only the Yellow Emperor (see page 97) who liked to perform outdoors. The painter-poet Wang Wei, "sitting alone among the secluded bamboos ... play[s] the zither and whistle[s] on and on",[2] while Li Bai's friend, the poet Meng Haoran, also felt the need to "take up a zither and play",[3] surrounded by lotus flowers and bamboos.

It will be useful, in structuring the discussion, to make a rough distinction between 'engagement with' and 'intervention in' nature. When I walk through a forest for pleasure, I am engaging with nature; when I chop down trees for firewood, I am intervening. It is, of course, impossible to engage without having some effects, without leaving marks. But only in the case of intervention are these effects intended. The man who hunts deer for pleasure and the gamekeeper who culls them have a similar effect on the deer population. But only in the second case is the intervention the point of the shooting, and hence an intervention in my sense.

In this and the next chapter, we will discuss engagements – for example, walking, swimming, recreational hunting and other pursuits through which people actively engage with nature. Later, we turn our attention to interventions in nature – to farming and gardening, for instance, and to environmental activism.

Being outdoors

Daoists spend a lot of time outdoors. Is this just because they like to? Or does the mood of Daoism call for engagement with nature? The answer is that, for Daoists, engagement is essential to the aspiration of convergence with nature. In a metaphor that might have come from a Daoist text, the film-maker and nature writer Roger Deakin praises "the poet/swimmer, who allows things to swim into his ken", a person both "active and passive", who "immerses himself in the natural world and takes part in its existence".[4] Deakin writes from experience; his first book, *Waterlog*, being a chronicle of his swims – in lakes, rivers, moats – throughout Britain. He understood well how doing something, like swimming, in a natural environment transforms the activity.

As a university student, I played saxophone in a band. Late one night, returning after a gig at a wedding reception, I stopped the car, took my saxophone into a field bathed in moonlight and blew until dawn. Twice that night, then, I played saxophone – but this single bland description elides two entirely different experiences. The one was a raucous experience in a public space shared with a hundred revellers; the other a private and tranquil one in a space shared only with a couple of cows. Or consider walking: there are languages which, more nuanced than English, prevent speakers from using a single verb for walking to work, walking the dog round the block, and walking through forests or mountains. In all three cases, the leg movements may be similar, but there the resemblance ends.

But how is an activity transformed when performed outdoors, and how might this nurture a person's convergence with nature? Like Zhuangzi's swimmer who "follows the course of the water itself without making any private one of [his] own" (Z 19), Deakin's poet/swimmer is receptive and pliant, his actions and moods spontaneously responding to the currents, waves, breezes, views, animal calls or whatever that impinge or announce themselves. Out there on the lake, things happen in a way they don't at the indoor swimming pool: things that constantly invite responsive, creative negotiations with an environment. There's a contrast here with more ruggedly purposeful swimmers, intent on getting from A to B or on clocking up X lengths of a pool. They, too, are alert, but only to obstacles and whatever else affects achievement of their goal. Instead, the engagement of the poet/swimmer – or the poet/walker, the poet/saxophonist – testifies to the mindful reverie of Daoist attunement to nature.

In reverie, as we have seen, a person glides easily from one thing to another, sensitive to the intimacies of connections. For Daoists, things are points of intersection in webs of experience: this is why mindful reverie is awareness of things as they are. Through engagement with natural environments this awareness is heightened. Walking through a forest, the trees, paths, flowers and creatures get "opened into one another" (Z 2), so as to form around the person who moves among them a fluid unity. As the walker descends from the forest, the way that the hill protects a farmhouse, attracts a covering of cloud, provides a route for deer, and lets streams flow into a river below becomes clear. To experience the hill in these and other aspects that unfold for the walker is to appreciate it as a site that 'gathers' a whole environment around it.[5] The walker allows the hill to show up for what it is and, by participating in nature, he or she acts in Zhuangzi's words as "the springtime of beings" (Z 5).

It became apparent in Chapter 9 that appreciation and enjoyment of the natural world, its beauties included, is a dimension of a convergent attunement to nature. This appreciation, without active engagement in the world, remains stunted, since such appreciation demands sensitivity to ambience or atmosphere. It is possible, occasionally, for someone who only sits and stares to take in the ambience and character of a place – but this appreciation is parasitic on engaged experience.

Only those who have walked through a forest can, later, get a sense of the forest's character just by looking at it from outside or above.

Ambience is important in the appreciation of nature for two reasons. First, the character or atmosphere of a place may itself be a focus of enjoyment and attention. What a place *feels like* – hard though it may be to describe – can matter more to people, and live longer in their memories, than this or that object they experienced there. Certainly appreciation of a surrounding environment is not reducible to enjoyment of its constituent bits.

Indeed – and here is the second reason – a sense of a place's ambience is typically a precondition of appreciative attention to particular things. Earlier today I was walking through an area of jungle, my attention drawn to some beautiful palm fronds and to the gentle murmurings of babbler birds. But it would not have been so drawn in a different context, for these sights and sounds stand out for attention – take on significance – through their location in the larger ambience of the jungle. The same fronds, glimpsed in a hotel lobby, would occasion no response and mean nothing. Engaged "immersion in a milieu",[6] emphasises one writer, is crucial for true sensitivity towards the flora and fauna that belong there.

Engagement, environment and convergence

These remarks on engaging with nature bear on the theme of convergence. An engaged participant is not a mere spectator for whom forests, rivers and mountains are 'scenery' to look at through a car or aeroplane window. A forest, for a person immersed in it, alert to its ambience and 'feel', is not an indifferent and external world. There is connection, a "felt relationship",[7] with the forest, even if it is sensed as dangerous or mysterious.

But there is a more radical point to make about convergence, engagement and environment. Put starkly: it is only through engagement with places that they become environments. A passage from the *Zhuangzi* helps make the point:

> Chomping the grass and drinking the waters, prancing and jumping over the terrain – this is the true inborn nature of horses. Even if given fancy terraces and great halls, they would have no use for them. (Z 9)

The contrast here is between a place, a 'terrain' of grassland and water, in which the horses engage and are at home, and other places, like palaces, which are alien since the animals cannot express their equine nature in them. In one sense of 'environment', only the former constitutes an environment for the horses. For, in this sense, a creature's environment is not a geographical area, measured in square metres, but a place where it knows its way about, understands how to act, and which has significance for it. An environment – like the horses' terrain of grass and river – is where a creature is 'at home', a place replete with meaning for it.

What is true of horses is true of people. A passage from Michael Morpurgo's novel *Running Wild* describes how for Will, a boy taken deep into the Indonesian rainforest on the back of an elephant fleeing from the 2004 tsunami, the jungle becomes an environment. For he gradually learns "a different way of being altogether, a new and uncomplicated kind of existence", and experiences "a growing familiarity with the jungle ... the world [he] now depended on." Will starts to "feel a kinship with this world ... no longer a stranger in this place" – not least because he now knows what is and isn't edible, what creatures to avoid. More generally, he has learned, like his elephant friend, "to live in rhythm with the jungle". In doing so, Will himself undergoes a "transformation" and is no longer "the same person" he had been back in England.[8]

None of this could have happened to Will had he been – like an eco-tourist – just a spectator of the jungle scene. For it is through engaged agency in the world around him – his search for food and water, his precarious relationships with the resident animals – that the jungle has become a domain of significance where he knows his way about, and it has thereby become his environment.

The dependence of environments on engagement means that, without engagement, there cannot be convergence. Without engagement there are no environments to converge with – no places imbued with a significance which allows for intimacy with them, no places in which to be at home. Without participation in nature by creatures and people, there would, to recall Zhuangzi's words, be "nothing selected out from it all" to constitute their environments (Z 2).

But the dependence of environments on engaged creatures is complemented by those creatures' dependence on environments. In the terminology of Chapter 6, there is 'co-dependence' here. For a creature to have a life, it must have an environment – a place or milieu where it knows its way about, where things are meaningful and matter to it, where it can express itself. When Zhuangzi's horses are captured, penned in a stall and forced into unnatural behaviour, they in effect cease to be creatures with lives, for they are without an environment in which to engage with any understanding. That's partly why, as the text tells us, more than half of the horses drop dead (Z 9).

Creatures depend on environment in the further sense that what they are like – who they are – is inseparable from their engagement with environments. Will, in Morpurgo's story, is 'transformed' when the jungle becomes his environment. There is not, for the Daoist, a self that may be identified and described independently of the world that is present to experience. So people who engage with the natural world are doubly convergent – doubly intimate – with the environments which then open up for them. Without them, there would be no environments, no spheres of significance. But without these spheres of significance, there would be no them either. Engagement is the overcoming in practice of the dualism between people and the world which the Daoist sage, we saw, also rejected at a theoretical level.

Finally, the convergence which engagement enables adds an important dimension to the sage's mindfulness and appreciation of nature. In being mindful of an environment, the sage is alert to his intimate engagement with it – to his own presence as something that both shapes and is shaped by the environment in which he participates. This intimacy then becomes a further focus of sober joy and appreciation. The mindful person take pleasure not only in the forest environment, but also in his or her having the forest *as* an environment. When Tao Qian returns to the countryside after living in the "dust-filled trap" of the city, it is not only nature that he celebrates, but also his having "got back again to nature", his renewed presence in his garden and village. A later poet, Han Yu, enjoys the mountain stream, but his enjoyment is in part reflexive:

> I walked barefoot on its stones,
> The water splashing noisily, my gown
> billowing in the wind.
> Life is just so easy to love
> when it is like this.[9]

This pleasure in the effect of the stones and the wind on his feet and legs is also an example of a prominent Daoist theme that deserves further exploration – attention to the body's presence in an environment.

'The Daoist body'

Swimmers, hikers and other people actively engaged outdoors are typically aware of their bodies – a springiness or fatigue in the legs, say. Sometimes an effect on the body is a goal of an outdoor activity: a person swims in order to relax her tense muscles; another goes climbing of a weekend to help him 'get into shape'. And sometimes care or cultivation of the body is the very focus of engaging with nature.

Bodily cultivation – through qigong (chi kung) or taiji (tai chi), for example – is a significant component in Chinese culture at large, but is given special emphasis in Daoist tradition. Indeed, Daoism has been characterised as "biospiritual cultivation"[10] and, by a scholar who is an ordained Daoist priest, a "tuning of the body".[11] These are characterisations, in the first instance, of later or 'religious' Daoism, which enjoined various disciplines of the body – dietary, sexual, ascetic. But concern for the body is there in the early classics too. Kristofer Schipper (the scholar/priest just mentioned) even goes on to say that Laozi's "thought springs from the religion of the body". Certainly, the *Daodejing* invites people to "value" and "love" their bodies, and to honour the body above wealth and fame (D 13, 44). Similarly, Zhuangzi endorses an earlier sage's command to "keep your body whole" and advises attention to the "central meridian" (*du*) that runs down the back and controls the flow of energy so as to "maintain our bodies" (Z 3, 23).

Two questions are raised by this emphasis on bodily cultivation. First, why this emphasis? Second, why should the body be cultivated, in significant part, through engagement with the natural world?

It is sometimes suggested that Daoism's rejection of a dualistic divide between mind and body – and hence of any privileging of the first over the second – is responsible for its attention to care of the body. But this can't be right. In ancient Greece and India, too, care of the body was a main component in techniques for leading a good life, despite the prevalence in those civilisations of dualistic accounts of mind versus body – Plato's, for instance, or that of the Samkhya-Yoga school.

More important than the issue of whether mind/spirit is a different kind of entity from the body is that of the range of relationships between mind/spirit and body. Are these, as later Western thinkers tended to suppose, of a merely causal kind – scratches bringing about pain, fear inducing perspiration, and the like? We know that, in China, further relationships were proposed – the 'correlatives' or 'correspondences' of physical phenomena with mental or moral qualities. This system, I suggested in Chapter 5, is an elaboration of the deep insight that physical, bodily features may be *expressive* of psychological, moral qualities. In the present context, the implication is that a properly cultivated, whole and vital body is an expression of a person's virtue, of his or her *de*.

Other things being equal, the virtues of the sage are expressed or manifested in bodily comportment that is beautiful, graceful, disciplined, modest and pliant. This is why Zhuangzi regards it as *problematic* that a man of undoubted virtue and charisma should be "ugly enough to frighten the whole world'. It is a puzzle, in effect, how virtue can fail to show itself in "external form", and why "inner" harmony is not always reflected by "outer" harmony (Z 5). Zhuangzi's own solution to this problem is unclear, but the important thing is his recognition of a concordance between virtue and the bodily, exceptions to which call for explanation. He would, I suspect, have concurred with Ludwig Wittgenstein's remark that "the human body is the best picture of the human soul".[12]

This explanation of the importance which Daoists attach to care of the body can coexist with a more familiar one in terms of achieving a 'wonderful old age' and a 'good death', as Schipper puts it.[13] Indeed, it lends depth to this idea. What is important in old age, for it to be 'wonderful', is not so much to remain fighting fit as to recognise it as the prime time of life for exercising Daoist virtues – for example, a humility and equanimity that are more difficult to practise during one's youth. And a good death is not a heroic or painless one, but the closure of a life which has become – and been seen to become – a life of virtue.

Why – aside from certain obvious conveniences – should cultivation of the body also be an engagement with natural environment? I do a sort of home-brewed tai chi most days, and I find that this, like my saxophone playing of bygone years, is an activity that is transformed when done outdoors, by a river bank or on a beach rather than in a gym. This comparison of playing music and cultivating the body is worth pursuing. Much of what the Yellow Emperor experienced when performing music in the wilds (Z 14) – the spontaneity of the sounds he made; the unforced responsiveness to surrounding elements; joy at the sense of a Way coursing through everything, oneself included – transfers to bodily disciplines that engage with nature.

A frequently employed metaphor is that of a *rhythm* belonging to musical and bodily practices which keeps time with a much greater rhythm. Authors variously write of an "embodying rhythm that joins with the Way of Heaven"[14] and of a "tuning of the body" that reflects "the rhythmic ways of the *Dao*". Tai chi and related exercises, it is said, enable "integration into the cosmic rhythm".[15]

Such metaphors relate cultivation of the body to an important Daoist discourse. *Dao*, as we saw in Chapters 6 and 7, does its gentle work through the rhythmic regularities of the seasons, night and day, the tides, and so on – rhythms that a farmer, long-haul traveller or boatman ignores at his or her peril. Ignores at a price, anyway – the price paid by someone who acts artificially, out of time with the natural beat of the world. Bodily exercise in a natural environment helps one to keep this beat; it is "a way of setting the body to [a] music"[16] which echoes a larger harmony. Such exercise in effect helps human beings to emulate the natural integration in their environments enjoyed by animals – which is why, in ancient documents like the *Daoyin tu* ('Gymnastics Chart'), particular exercises are given names like 'crane spreading wings' or 'monkey leaping'.[17]

For Daoists, then, tai chi and other disciplines of the body are, when practised outdoors and in engagement with nature, ways of experiencing integration with the natural world – responsive as they are to natural rhythms, like the pounding of waves or the rolling of clouds, which suffuse one's environment.[18] They are, of course, ways of moving the body, but they are also experiences of being moved. For, when performed effortlessly and with economy and grace, these disciplines inspire a sense of being "opened . . . into the single energy that is the world" (Z 22).

Wilderness, wildness, wildlife

"Every walk", proclaimed Thoreau, "is a sort of crusade". This sounds an exaggerated way of describing some of the walks – through gentle countryside, say – envisaged in the preceding chapter. And, indeed, it is only walks of a more rugged kind, through wilderness areas, which Thoreau has in mind. His remark registers a yearning for an "absolute wildness" which "no civilisation can endure", for it is from "dismal swamps", not cultivated parks or farms, that he "derive[s] his subsistence". "Give me . . . the wilderness", Thoreau pleads.[1]

Here is an early and vivid statement of the now-popular idea that engagement with wilderness is the authentic way of engaging with nature. Gentler, less raw encounters with more 'civil' landscapes – swimming in a local river, say, or a walk along its bank – are not, in this view, significant engagements with natural environments. For us moderns, the idea goes, convergence with nature is re-convergence with the wildernesses prowled by our distant ancestors. Would the Daoist endorse this understanding of convergence?

The wild

At first glance, equating engagements with nature and with wilderness gets support from Daoist writings and art. The 'primitivist' chapters of the *Zhuangzi* (Z 8-11) contain passages that appear to recall a golden age of "perfect virtue" when "the mountains had no paths . . . the marshes had no boats or barges", and:

The birds and beasts clustered with each other, the grasses and trees grew unhampered . . . People lived together with the birds and beasts, bunched together with all things. (Z 9)

Daoist-inspired paintings of travellers in remote mountains, or of people perched on crags, seem to testify to a wilderness ideal.

But care is needed here. The golden age invoked by the *Zhuangzi*, echoing the *Daodejing*, is not that of primitive life pursued in an uncultivated wilderness, but of a simple agrarian society where people plough, raise livestock and live in villages. The testimony of Daoist painting and poetry is mixed. Pictures and verses which represent wild places are matched by ones – like the poems of Tao Qian – which celebrate more bucolic landscapes. A closer look at paintings which appear to depict remote wilderness areas often reveals signs of human dwelling – temples, huts, bridges, boats.

It is true, though, that Daoist texts are without the hostility to wilderness that was once characteristic of Christianity – and indeed of early Buddhism, where a utopian life is located in "villages, towns and cities", with their "parks and groves", and not among "reeds and bushes" (see *Digha Nikaya* [Long Discourses], Sutra 26). It is hard, certainly, to imagine a Daoist sage experiencing the guilt felt by Petrarch when in 1336, from the summit of Mt Ventoux, he found himself enjoying the panoramic view of merely 'earthly things'.[2]

While there is no Daoist hostility to wilderness, however, nor is 'the wilderness experience' privileged by Daoists over engagement with human landscapes, with cultivated environments. As will emerge later, in Daoist writings it is the *garden* – as much as or more than a wilderness – which is an epitome of significant experience of nature.

"That may be," someone is likely to retort, "but – whatever the texts might say – surely Daoists *ought* to privilege the experience of wilderness. Nothing less would accord with their antipathy to contrivance, and their corresponding praise of spontaneity and simplicity."

This retort is unconvincing. To begin with, it is guilty of a confusion noted in Chapter 5 when discussing Daoist conceptions of nature. Daoists are second to none in appreciating the importance of experiencing wildness, of engaging with beings and processes which owe nothing to human contrivance. But wildness is not wilderness. A few weeks ago, I encountered a very young cobra which, hissing and rearing its hood, displayed all its wildness. But this encounter took place, not in a remote jungle, but in the well-tended grounds of a Sri Lankan guest house. Wildness, to recall the earlier discussion, is a 'process' as evident in a small wood at the edge of a village, or even in a guest house garden, as in those regions we call wildernesses. A patch of lawn, remarked Roger Deakin, is 'a jungle in miniature' to someone alert to the wildness of small creatures.

Some readers will still feel, however, that surely it is only in engagement with wilderness that a person fully exercises the uncontrived naturalness, spontaneity and simplicity of the Daoist sage. Only someone who has heard 'the call of the wild' and obeyed a summons to go 'back to nature' can authentically relate to the natural world.

This feeling is rooted in a conception of human beings as fundamentally wild creatures whose primitive impulses and instincts, though suppressed in civilised life, should be given expression. The conception is familiar from the pages of Thoreau, Freud and D. H. Lawrence, and is explicit in John Fowles' call to release 'the wild green-man' who is 'part of our own psyches'. In this vein, the author of a book entitled *How to be Wild* refers to human beings as possessing, deep down, an "ancient wild self . . . a hunter-gatherer soul". Because we are "evolved for the wild", "living a wilder life is a better way to live".[3]

The Daoist sage has little sympathy for this view of human beings, rejecting its picture of a real, inner and wilder self struggling to be released. A person's self, for Daoists, is an experiential route through the world, not something that has an identity or substance independently of the way the world is experienced by this person. Clearly the routes through the world that most people take today are very different from those of our distant ancestors, so that no sense attaches to the atavistic idea that, *really*, our selves are still the souls or psyches of hunter-gatherers or wild green-men.

Moreover, the Daoist will add, there is no need at all to embrace the wilderness ideal in order to honour and practise the virtues of naturalness, spontaneity and simplicity. Daoists look back with nostalgia to a time when human life was less contrived, less fettered by rules and conventions, less rigidly goal-directed. But this is not nostalgia for life led in the wild by creatures in a pre-civilised state of nature, rather for an age before the emergence of an obsession with rites, principles and technical knowledge. When Laozi (D 80) and Zhuangzi (Z 12) reject the introduction of hi-tech devices and contraptions, this is to preserve an untroubled form of peasant life, not an existence that pre-dated human settlement and agriculture.

It would be wrong, too, to suppose that the sage's spontaneity can only be properly exercised by people whose lives emulate those of their wild, green-man ancestors. Indeed, to suppose this is to fail to "distinguish a *wrong* kind of spontaneity, the surrender to passions that distort awareness, from the right [Daoist] kind, responsiveness in the impersonal calm when vision is most lucid".[4] The spontaneity of the sage may be practised just as well in a garden as in a remote mountain terrain.

The thought that the Daoist call for *simplicity* harks back to a wilder, pre-civilised age may sound more plausible. The *Daodejing* enjoins a "return to being unhewn wood (*pu*)" (D 28) – a metaphor, it is sometimes suggested, for the simplicity of life in an unadulterated natural state. But this is a strange suggestion. Unhewn wood (or the uncarved block) is a metaphor in some contexts for *dao* itself, for what has yet to become divided up into separate, nameable things (D 32). Elsewhere, it is a symbol for release from desires. "Nameless unhewn wood is but freedom from desire" (D 37). So, someone who 'returns to being unhewn wood' is 'on the Way', in accord with *dao*, and someone who has achieved equanimity. This is not a return to a primal state of nature, to a wild condition where impulse and instinct prevail.

A similar point applies to Laozi's call for a "return to the state of childhood" (D 28). This is not a summons to retrieve, impossibly, a stage of life that preceded enculturation. Rather, it enjoins us to respect "innocence, plainness and simplicity".[5] (Nor, it is worth adding, is the suggestion that the child we should emulate is a feral one, a Mowgli-like creature at home only in the company of wild beasts.)

The Daoist sage might well be found trekking through remote mountains, crossing arctic wastes, or meditating in jungle clearings. But he might equally be found walking round his garden, strolling across bridges over a river running through his village, or sitting in reverie at the edge of a pasture. Engagement with the natural world may well be with wilderness, but this is not something that the Daoist privileges over engagement with the countryside and other human landscapes.

Wildlife and hunting

The mention just now of wild animals prompts the question of how, for the Daoist, these should be engaged with by people.

Let's begin by considering a close cousin of the 'wild self' approach. In this view, we should engage with wild animals in the manner of our wild ancestors – primarily, by hunting them. In the words of the poet-philosopher of hunting, José Ortega y Gasset, hunting is the authentic and "generic way of being a man".[6] This proposition is endorsed by an author who tells us on a website that he won the Sacred Trophy of the Outdoors Writing Association of America.[7] He goes on to speak of hunting as a "fundamental instinct", a "spiritual experience", which "connects us most profoundly with animals" and helps us to "fall in love with nature". So "deeply rooted in human nature" is this instinct that we can only conclude that "God made us to be hunters".

This 'hunter porn' – as it's been called by a writer not immune to its seductions[8] – has popular resonance these days. In Britain, hunting has become an increasingly popular and demotic pursuit over the last few decades. Thirty million pheasants, for example, are bred to be shot each year. And people who hunt frequently speak the rhetoric of 'hunter porn' – 'closeness to nature', 'connecting with animals' and the like – in defence of their hobby.

Hunting defended in these terms needs distinguishing from killing animals for the sole purpose of eating them, or for other practical goals such as livestock protection and culling unsustainable herds. (People who hunt for pleasure, or to follow the 'generic way of being a man', tend, of course, to invoke such practical purposes in front of audiences that might otherwise frown upon their enthusiasm.) In a pronounce-ment of Ortega's, cited on many shooters' websites, "one does not hunt in order to kill, one kills in order to have hunted". Hunting pur-sued in this spirit is our present concern – hunting not for any practical purpose, but as, allegedly, a pre-eminently authentic engagement with wildlife, securely rooted in human nature.

Hunting for pleasure was a pastime of rulers in ancient China just as in Rome and Persia. The great Qin emperor, Shi Huang, constructed Shang-lin park near his capital, Xianyang, as a hunting preserve, and rulers of the Han empire, which succeeded the Qin in 210 BCE, con-tinued to hunt there. Han poets testify that the hunting was ferocious and on a huge scale, leaving "the stiff corpses of the slain, bird and beast, glisten[ing] like tide-washed pebbles on a beach".[9]

Daoist texts do not explicitly comment on imperial hunting or express opposition to killing animals for food, clothing and so on. Zhuangzi, we know, liked to fish. But there's an interesting passage in the *Zhuangzi* which calls for moderation and the use of simple methods in hunting and trapping. Clever crossbows, traps, nets, snares and other devices throw into "disorder" and "confusion" the "birds of the sky . . . the fish of the waters . . . [and] the beasts of the woodlands". More generally, the passage condemns technologically sophisticated "cunning and deception" in the practice of hunting and killing of animals (Z 10). It is hard to imagine Zhuangzi enthusing over the high-velocity rifles, with their night-vision sights, in the arsenal of today's shooters.

More important, it is impossible to imagine him sympathising with modern-day 'hunter porn'. For Daoists, this rhetoric is doubly guilty of fantasy. For a start, it is a special case of the 'wild self' proposal. The presentation of hunting as our 'fundamental instinct' or 'generic way of being' subscribes to the myth of an essential nature or self, bequeathed by our hunter-gatherer ancestors, that still lurks within us and seeks release from repression. This idea that all human beings, except for the small number who hunt animals, are frustrated victims of repression is, from a Daoist perspective, merely quaint.

Quaint, too, and equally fantastical, is the pretence by modern-day hunters that their pursuit is, in any serious sense, the one engaged in by their distant forebears. On autumn mornings in Malta, unshaven men, rifles in hand, wearing camouflaged clothing, jump into camouflaged pick-up trucks accompanied by their fearsome dogs. To all appearances, they are off to do battle with a marauding pack of wolves or an invading herd of elephants. In fact, they are off to shoot turtle doves. There is fantasy in their very description of themselves as 'hunters', and certainly in their invocation of a millennia-old tradition.

As Daoists will point out, what gives to an activity its identity is not simply overt behaviour – picking up a weapon and killing something with it – but also its place in a wider context of experience and perspectives. Only at a superficial level is the contemporary Maltese 'hunter' re-living the life of hunter-gatherer ancestors. His world is not their world, and what he does is without the significance of what they did. Whatever he is doing, it is not connecting with animals and the natural world as they once did.

For the Daoist, then, 'hunter porn' is a literature of fantasy, and hunters who take it seriously are failing to see things as they are. This is a failure of mindfulness – and not the only failure of which hunters are guilty. On several occasions in this book, attention has been drawn to Zhuangzi's and Liezi's call to recognise and respect the perspectives of animals. Liezi reminds us that animals do not exist for the sake of human pleasures, while Zhuangzi refers us to an order in the animal kingdom before this was destroyed by the excesses of hunters and trappers. The texts frequently remind readers of the mindless, culpable ignorance complicit in people's treatment of animals. Ignorance, for example, of the number of doves which must die in order for just a few to be caught (L 8), or of the suffering caused to horses and birds through people's blindness to their needs and natures (Z 9, 19). They remind us, too, that the desires and "intelligence of beasts and birds [are] by nature similar to man's" and that "they wish as much as we do to preserve their lives" (L 2). In older and better times, "people lived together with the birds and beasts" (Z 9, L 2). The implication is that people mindful of the lives of animals could not, like the hunters who have helped destroy this communion with birds and beasts, casually and merrily end those lives. Do – *can* – people kill a deer or a dove with gusto if they are mindful of the creature's life in a family bound by ties of affection, even love?

There is irony in the charge that hunters are not mindful of animals, since a popular boast in 'hunter porn' is precisely the intensely heightened attention to creatures and their environment needed by the hunter. Ortega speaks of the "perpetual alertness" of the hunter, in an environment where everything is "loaded with meaning". But the same passage betrays how different the hunter's attentiveness is from the mindfulness exercised by the Daoist sage. Ortega's hunter, close to his prey, "sees each thing functioning as facility or difficulty, as risk or protection".[10] Everything is seen pragmatically and instrumentally, in relation to the hunter's objective of killing an animal. There is nothing here of the 'indifferent', 'impartial' reverie in the presence of nature which characterises the sage's mindfulness.

Guns, cameras, companions

"In the evening I watched hundreds of wild ducks . . . I was sorry that I had not brought my gun with me, but . . . I did the next best thing and watched them with my binoculars." So writes the author of a book about his life in the jungles of southern Sri Lanka. The book expresses a zest for killing animals ("I have done my bit for Ceylon by killing every viper I have ever come across"), often in the language of 'hunter porn' (there'll be 'no real men' left if the Buddhists manage to get hunting banned). At the same time, other passages, and the author's drawings of animals and birds, demonstrate sensitivity to, and compassion for, various creatures.[11]

This complexity of attitude and behaviour is not uncommon among hunters. (I remember being surprised by it as a child when I leafed through a book, *The Pleasures of Pig-Sticking*, by a former Bengal Lancer who purported to love wild creatures, even the unfortunate pigs.) And there are many cases where hunters – changing, as it were, from poaching to game-keeping – turn to other ways of engaging with wildlife: photography, tracking, bird-watching, ecotourism, and so on. In Malta, a Green Party slogan enjoins the turtle-dove hunters to shoot with cameras, not with guns. Quite a few have listened. And, today, many more people – ones never attracted to hunting – enjoy birding, wildlife photography and other less lethal forms of relating to wildlife.

Is there a Daoist 'line' on such activities? The Daoist, we know, may be found in wild areas, but is unlikely to be carrying a gun or a spear. But how about a camera, a twitcher's book of sightings, binoculars, or some other accoutrement of the modern wildlife enthusiast?

The Daoist attitude towards these forms of engagement will depend on the tone and manner in which they are pursued. In his book *The Peregrine*, J. A. Baker describes in relentless detail his one-year communion with the bird of the title, one he watched and followed each day. No reason for this behaviour is given beyond a wish "to be part of the outward life" of natural environments. No gain, no fame, no advantage, is expected from following the bird. That is why, perhaps, readers of the book recognise sincerity in the author's attempt to "preserve a unity, binding together the bird, the watcher, and the place that holds them both".[12]

But if this author's way of engagement with a wild creature is one of convergence with the natural world, other ways are less so. There are two connected dangers which the Daoist perceives in modern wildlife enthusiasms. One is that wildlife becomes a resource – not for food or fur, but for entertainment, the satisfaction of curiosity, or game-playing among people who compete to sight and record the most species. Zhuangzi and Liezi, who disliked animals being put on show in palaces, would not condone their being turned into a spectacle, even in their natural habitats.

Since most people find some creatures more showy, entertaining and interesting than others, a second danger is that their experience of animals is distorted by partiality. Twitchers may be intent on a rarely sighted bird but indifferent to the familiar ones around them. Photographers and eco-tourists may hardly notice the unassuming animals which they pass as their jeeps head for where a leopard has been spied. Mindful attention to creatures, Daoists will remind us, calls for a quiet responsiveness against which modern, frenzied styles of engagement with wildlife easily militate.

At the end of *The Peregrine*, the author quietly stands close to the falcon as it sleeps, unafraid, on an old sea-wall – proof of the "impalpable bond" that has grown between the two of them. Such companionship between people and wild creatures is an engagement in a Daoist key. Liezi writes that, because he neither indulges them nor "thwarts" them, the birds and animals which "roam in [his] garden . . . and sleep in his yard", without a desire to return to distant habitats, "regard [him] as one of themselves" (L 2). And the story that he and Zhuangzi tell of a time when men and animals lived together and 'walked side by side' depicts an ideal to which a person may aspire.

Most of us lack the determination, charisma, gift or courage that enables the communion with wild animals enjoyed by the author of *The Peregrine*, St Francis of Assisi, Dr Dolittle, or primatologists like Dian Fossey and Jane Goodall. But even in our modern urban societies, there are opportunities for coming to know, and be known, by wild creatures – the birds, hedgehogs, squirrels and foxes that people feed or welcome to their gardens; in some countries even the cobras for which bowls of milk are left out.

One of the happier neologisms of recent years is 'companion animal' as a name for pets. These, by definition, are not wildlife – though, as with the animals that no longer wish to stray far from Liezi's garden, the line between the two is not sharp. It would in any case betray confusion to condemn the keeping of animals as companions, as some environmental ethicists do, on the ground that animals should be left to be wild. This is the confusion, once more, between wildness and wilderness. Domestic cats do not live in a wilderness, but much of their behaviour – mating, mothering, hunting, fighting – is as wild, as untutored by human beings, as that of their feral cousins.

So, companionship between people and their pets is also, in its way, an engagement with the wild, and one that belongs in a wider convergence with nature. Liezi, it is reported, regarded his pigs as pets and, partly perhaps because of this, "treated all things as equally his kin" (L 2). He would, I suspect, endorse Milan Kundera's reference to dogs as 'joyful ambassadors from the animal kingdom' – for, like all good ambassadors, they further contact with and understanding of what might seem to be an alien realm.

12

Intervening in nature

Walking, swimming in rivers, shooting doves and other engagements with nature have their impact on the natural world. But this is not usually their purpose, as it is with what I call 'interventions' in nature. In the modern world, people intervene in nature in many different ways and for many different reasons. They extract materials from the earth, grow cereals, raise cattle, turn heaths into gardens, participate in conservation projects, and so on. Profit, satisfaction of consumer demands, pleasure, a work ethic and environmentalist commitments are among the motives for interventions in the natural world.

How do interventions – a representative sample of them, at any rate – look from a Daoist perspective? There is, in Daoist literature, no blanket condemnation of intervention, no Manichean divide between the "glorious world [of] unspoiled nature" and one "defiled" by the industry of man, that "lewd bare-buttocked ape".[1] Daoists do not speak of human beings as "a planetary disease . . . an absolute pathogen".[2] Daoism, though, as we have seen, has its 'moods', shared by many contemporary nature writers. These include a nostalgia for intimacy with nature, and a sense of its mystery, both of which have been eroded in human societies. This erosion, Daoists think, is in part the product of ways in which human beings have physically intervened in nature, and is not simply the result of changing beliefs or attitudes. The Daoist concern is not to pass judgement on human history, but to decide which kinds of intervention by a person are consonant with being 'on the Way', with exercising *de*. Could a Daoist, for example, run a factory farm, make gardens, or become an environmental activist?

Industry and technology

Among interventions whose purpose is to produce goods for human consumption, a rough distinction can be made between 'industry' and 'agriculture'. Industrial intervention is the removal of materials from the earth or ocean – through mining, logging or oil-drilling, for example – for processing and conversion into consumables. Agricultural intervention is primarily the use of land for growing crops and raising animals which yield edible products. Here, we are concerned firstly with industrial intervention. (The distinction is not sharp: trees logged for the paper mill may have been purpose-grown and have, as a by-product, something that animals or people eat.)

Daoist texts voice no opposition to drawing upon nature for materials used in the production of things. Indeed, some of the heroes in these texts are craftsmen who work on materials they have themselves extracted – the bell-stand maker, for example, who goes into the forest for the wood he needs (Z 19). In the *Liezi*, 'stealing' from heaven and earth – in order, say, to obtain wood and clay for building a house – is explicitly approved (L 1). But the same passages also indicate conditions under which interventions are acceptable. Zhuangzi's craftsman carefully attends to the character and demands of his raw materials before starting work on them. Similarly, Liezi explains that legitimate 'stealing' is informed by a sense that what is taken is "begotten by heaven" and, in effect, always belongs, not to oneself, but to heaven.

Daoist interventions in nature – patient, reflective, modest, responsive to the materials 'stolen', sensible of the mysterious 'ownership' of what the earth yields – bear little resemblance to the interventions of modern industrial technology. These interventions are required by and complicit in the frenzied, hyperactive character of modern, developed societies. Industrial intervention is powered by demands for more and cheaper goods, and licensed by an entrenched vision of the natural world as something 'on tap' for human use.

The Daoist, we saw in Chapter 3, shares Martin Heidegger's understanding of this vision – that of 'technology', as he called it – as so thoroughly entrenched that other views of the world, other 'ways of revealing' it, are driven out. For all the rhetoric heard these days about the sanctity of nature, it is the enterprise of extracting oil, not the fate of sea birds or mangroves, which – everyone knows – easily prevails. In some cases, other ways of revealing are, quite literally, driven out: as when animals or indigenous people, with their own perspectives on the jungle or swamps they inhabit, are removed to make way for a dam or ranch.

One perspective that is driven out by modern industrial technology is the kind articulated by Zhuangzi and Liezi. Industrial intervention is without any sense of earth, wood, water, clay or oil being 'given' by, and finally 'owned' by, a mysterious source. In today's factories, which convert what the logger or oil driller supplies into products, there is no perception of 'joining what is heaven's to what is heaven's'.

Champions of industrial intervention may invoke utilitarian considerations, such as the satisfaction of consumer needs, but this was not always the case. One thinks, for example, of the Protestant tradition according to which, as John Locke put it in 1688, "God commanded man to labour" and gave the earth "to the use of the Industrious",[3] who thereby obeyed the divine will. A greater influence on twentieth-century industrialisation, and still with a resonance in today's developing economies, was a muscular ideology that appealed to communists, fascists and capitalists alike. In a variation on the 'green-man' myth, Oswald Spengler's ideal of the 'Faustian man' was a call, not to return to the wild, but to bring the wild, the law of the jungle, into industrial civilisation. Faustian man is a "beast of prey", governed by "carnivore ethics" and an indomitable "will to power". Despising a utilitarian, profit-seeking attitude towards nature, Faustian man's "destiny" is to "pit himself against" nature, "to enslave and harness her". His "passion has nothing to do with consequences", and everything to do with "building a world *oneself*", in effect becoming "*oneself* God".[4] As a like-minded contemporary of Spengler's put it, the authentic industrial worker is a "cybernetic storm-trooper", caught up in a "total mobilisation" of men and machines for the subjection of the natural world.[5]

The Daoist rejects each component in this vision of industrial intervention in nature. Faustian man, a 'Viking of the blood' struggling to break through his civilised carapace, is a virtual repetition – despite the different ideology he encapsulates – of the 'wild self' / 'green-man soul' rejected in the last chapter. The summons to 'build a world', to emulate a god, through imposing a will to power on nature contradicts the idea that human enterprise is dependent on a source that is not of human making. At the same time, this hubristic summons is a rejection of convergence, for there can be no yearning for convergence with a nature fit only to be 'harnessed and enslaved' by the industrial cousins of storm-troopers.

Daoists, then, are not found in logging or mining camps or in other places where, as the poet Gerard Manley Hopkins expressed it, men 'hack and rack' the earth. (Daoists of the time probably applauded the Qin dynasty general, Meng Tian, who confessed to the "crime" of building ramparts and ditches that had "cut through the earth's veins".[6]) But they will be found among craftsmen who, intervening in a gentler style, take wood, clay, reeds and other materials from nature to make things – chairs, bowls, mats – for everyday use. Daoists practise and encourage crafts not in the hope of instigating a global retreat from a modern to a medieval economy, but because craft may embody *de*, and be consonant with *dao*, in a way that industrial technology cannot.

Engaged experience of nature, I argued in Chapter 10, is essential to a right attunement to the natural world, to properly understanding and appreciating it. For Daoists, work offers engaged experience of an especially vital kind. This is why the craftsman's knowledge is privileged, in Daoist writings, over scholarly knowledge. It is what the wheelwright, as he chisels, "feels in the hand" and cannot be "put into words" that matters, not what his aristocratic employer is gleaning from books (Z 13). When using hand tools, like a chisel, the craftsman is alert not only to the details of wood or stone, but also engaged with it in a peculiarly concentrated and intimate way.

Alert and focused, but also flexibly responsive. A responsive sensitivity, for Daoists, is there right at the start, when the craftsman selects a tree or a rock to supply material on which to work. The bell-stand maker in the *Zhuangzi* explains how he sets about getting some suitable wood to work on:

> When I am going to make a bell-stand . . . I enter into the mountain forests, viewing the inborn heavenly nature of the

trees. My body arrives at a certain spot, and already I see the completed bell-stand there: only then do I apply my hand to it. Otherwise I leave the tree alone. (Z 19).

And this sensitivity continues during the work itself, for if the beauty and character of the material are to be exposed, the craftsman must resist working to a rigid plan that is immune to changing perceptions of the material's qualities.

Although the craftsman's purpose is a practical one – to make a bowl, say – this is properly achieved only through disinterested attention to materials. Zhuangzi's famous butcher, whose cleaver remains razor sharp after 19 years of carving, is a craftsman in his way – and he speaks for craftsmen in general when describing how he relies on "heaven's structuring" and is "guided by what is inherently so" in the carcasses he cuts up (Z 3).

As the butcher's remark implies, craftsmanship exercised in the spirit of *wu wei* manifests the virtue of humility as well as responsiveness. Unlike Faustian man, neither the butcher nor the bell-stand maker attributes to human achievement what is heaven's accomplishment. This is a main theme in a book by a twentieth-century Japanese champion of everyday crafts, Sōetsu Yanagi – a Zen Buddhist who appreciated Zen's debt to Daoism. A good potter or woodworker knows the extent of a successful work's "dependence on Other Power (*tariki-dō*)", and therefore "works more in grace than in his own power". In remarks with a Daoist resonance, Yanagi contrasts true and false craftworks, explaining that a work conveys truth when it "expound[s] in material form" that its source is not the maker's ego, but Other Power.[7] Rendered in a Daoist idiom, a tea bowl, say, has truth when it – like its maker and the process of its making – is 'on the Way'. In effect, it owes its beauty – like the natural landscapes discussed in Chapter 9 – to its exemplification of virtue.

Agriculture

Classical Chinese writers wrote little about industrial interventions in nature, for during their times (and for another two millennia) China's was an overwhelmingly agricultural economy. By the third century

BCE, in the Yellow and Yangzi river valleys, a sophisticated and regu-
lated agriculture had been developed based on farming by small, largely self-sufficient village communities. For example, in the 'well-field'
system admired by Mencius, families owned plots around an area of
common land for which the community was responsible.[8]

The importance of agriculture was reflected in the attention paid
to it by poets, like those who composed the *Book of Odes* (*Shijing*), and
by philosophers alike.[9] According to a first-century CE Han classification, one of the ten main schools of thought during earlier centuries
had been 'the Agricultural school'. Sections of the third-century BCE
compilation *Lüshi Chunqiu* ('Mr Lü's Spring and Autumn Annals'),[10]
were devoted to 'the value of agriculture', as were passages in works by
the Confucian thinkers Mencius and Dong Zhongshu (Tung Chung-
Shu). Remarks on farmers and farming are found, naturally, in Daoist
texts as well.

In these writings, agriculture is not treated solely as an economic
enterprise, to be pursued according to criteria of only cost and utility.
For their authors, farming is a form of culture, an 'agri-culture'. When
Mencius praises the 'well-field' system, this is because it encourages
friendship, mutual aid, equality and harmony among the plot owners.
For Mr Lü, the farmer's mode of life is a superior one – simple, unself-
ish, obedient – and in this lies 'the value of agriculture'. In the *Daodejing*, a simple farming community is admired, not for its productive
efficiency, but because the villagers "relish their food . . . feel comfortable in their homes . . . and delight in their customs", and have no urge
to leave or even to meet with people from neighbouring states (D 80).

The Daoist complaint against modern agricultural interventions is
that they have turned into a type of industry what once was a form of
culture. Farming no longer constitutes a distinctive life-world; instead
it has become incorporated into the world of industrial technology. It
takes on the features associated with industrial intervention – frenzy,
hubris, myopia – at the same time that it loses those characteristic of a
culture – respect for tradition, 'delight in customs', shared perceptions
of significance and goodness.[11]

On the radio a few mornings ago, a Lecturer in Agriculture
defended the construction of a milk factory in which 8,000 cows will
be enclosed, with no opportunity to graze outside. After all, he explained,

the only relevant criterion is the production of the greatest volume of milk at the lowest possible cost. This is in sharp contrast to an older attitude expressed in the words of a Polish farmer who, like Zhuangzi's peasant, fears the effects of new, intrusive technology. He prefers to remain with "the old ways [which] moved in harmony with the seasons, the sun, the weather". Even if this is "less efficient", it has other, more important, qualities, like "belonging to a history that attached itself to the land".[12]

The atrophy of a form of culture is also the degradation of environments in the sense discussed in Chapter 10 – spheres of significance that a person feels connected to and at home in. The traditional family farm was itself an environment, locked moreover into a larger environment of farming families, villagers, local retailers and consumers. The modern industrial farm is not an environment of this kind, nor part of one. Those who work in a factory farm contribute to a complex process of food production whose understanding has been relinquished to experts – agronomists, geneticists, nutritionists and so on. They have no relationship to the people who consume the final products – chicken nuggets, hamburgers – which derive from the stuffs into which poultry or cattle have been converted. The industrial farm is not a home but, like an office, somewhere to do a day's work before returning home. It is a kind of farm or 'agricultural operation' – stark, gleaming, often sinister – more apt to alienate the neighbouring village than to form a community with it.

In one respect, modern agricultural intervention represents a more total imposition of human will upon nature than is possible in other industries. In the *Zhuangzi*, a man is gently chided for attributing a human point of view to some pigs (Z 19). But at least he thinks they *have* a point of view worth considering, unlike battery farmers – or managers of CAFOs (Combined Animal Feeding Operations) – who not only provide the animals for processing into stuffs, but also treat the creatures themselves as stuff. Unlike the traditional farmer, who had to have regard for an animal's nature if it was to grow well, the industrial farmer profits by ignoring the creature's natural need to graze, peck, or indeed have space in which to move.

Liezi, it is reported, "served food to his pigs as if they were human and treated all beings as equally his kin" (L 2). For some fellow Daoists,

Liezi errs here on the side of anthropomorphism. But this is not an error comparable with that of absolute disregard for the integrity of living beings. Absolute, since no prejudice about animals could more completely obscure their nature than a perception of them as lumps of raw material.

Daoists, we have seen, are less likely to be found at sites of industrial intervention in nature than in places where older, gentler crafts are practised. Similarly, it is not where agri-business holds sway that the Daoist is found, but where the craftsman-like work of traditional farming is continued. Work such as laying a hedge or making a dry-stone wall to protect livestock, rather than erecting steel fences or concrete barriers. This is not out of an unrealistic ambition to reverse the development of the modern world and return it to a medieval, or perhaps 'well-field', economy. Such work is done, rather, out of a desire by individual men and women to farm in a manner expressive of Daoist virtues, one consonant with *dao*.

Daoists will prefer, like the Polish farmer, to farm in 'old ways' that are in harmony with – converge with – the rhythms of the seasons, sun and weather. Their animals, for example, will live outside when possible, knowing whether it is day or night, summer or winter, cloudy or clear. Daoists will want, as well, to be mindful of what they grow, its origin and its destination – to understand the process for themselves rather than surrendering to the knowledge of experts. Ideally, they will themselves plant, grow, harvest, prepare and bake. They will want this process to be embedded in an environment, a field of significance, which they share with others – neighbouring smallholders, their livestock and the animals that live in nearby woods and valleys; local villagers and other people who eat the food they grow.

The Daoist smallholder will want, finally, to intervene in nature, as Karl Marx put it, 'according to the laws of beauty'. Here, he will resemble the French peasant described by the novelist Jean Giono. This is a man whose work is "really something beautiful . . . His scythe never wavered . . . the necessary gestures came exact and perfectly timed . . . It was a joy to watch", for it was something done "for pleasure, for joy, for the sake of doing it well".[13] Here, in the effortless grace of bodily movement is an expression of the sober joy, appreciation of beauty, and spontaneity which distinguish someone who is 'on the Way'.

When Marx wrote of people "fashion[ing] things according to the laws of beauty", however, he also meant something redolent of a Daoist virtue already invoked in our discussion of intervention. Such people, Marx says, "produce according to the measure of every species" and know the "inherent standard" of each species.[14] In effect, people farm beautifully when they recognise and respect the integrity – the nature, the perspectives even – of seeds, plants, soil and animals. Ugly farming – in broiler batteries and monocultural corn-belts – is intervention that attends only to human needs and looks away from the good of other species of living things.

The Daoist garden

I've just come in to my study from doing some work in the garden: cutting back a hedge, weeding a patio. Farmers have to do similar work – but there's the difference: they *have to*, I don't. Farming, though it may be practised 'according to the laws of beauty', is still a practical intervention in nature, geared to the overall purpose of producing food. With certain exceptions such as kitchen gardens, gardens are not made or maintained in order to achieve any such practical or material goal. Gardening is one of a range of interventions in nature – including landscaping and environmental art – pursued for less tangible reasons, or perhaps simply 'for their own sake'.

Why do I garden? Maybe an answer will emerge from Daoist reflections on the virtues or otherwise of gardening and related interventions. It might seem that Daoists should be opposed to gardening. Certainly it seemed so to a group of students whom, their lecturer reports, reacted with outrage to a book that described the garden of a Daoist hermitage, where art had been applied to 'modifying' and 'assisting' nature. "A true nature lover", the students clearly felt, "would simply leave nature alone".[15] Surely, their reaction implied, the Daoist rejection of hubris entails rejection of culture's attempt to modify nature simply for human enjoyment.

Presumably the students would be still more outraged to learn that Daoism has been a prominent influence on the Chinese garden tradition. Though what we today recognise as the Chinese style did not emerge until centuries after the composition of the Daoist classics, the 'literati' gardens of the Tang and Song dynasties were expressive of Daoist, as well as Confucian, themes. Daoist priests were among the most important makers of gardens at popular scenic sites (*bajin*), and garden design inspired by Daoist sensibilities flourished again during the Ming and Qing dynasties.

During these periods, poems and essays – such as the eleventh-century 'Record of the Joy Garden' and 'Record of the Garden of Solitary Enjoyment' – emphasise that the garden, protected from 'the dust and grime' of the city, was a place of peace in which a person could engage in reverie and conduct himself 'without striving'. They allude, as well, to the garden as an environment for close, safe and tranquil observation of the natural workings of *dao* – processes of growth and decay, the effects of the seasons, metamorphosis, and so on.

That "great nature [may] be seen in a [new] way" through mindful attention to the garden is one reason why the opposition between nature and culture is challenged in the celebrated seventeenth-century work *Yuan Ye* ('The Craft of Gardens').[16] But to understand why the Daoist garden is a site where this opposition founders, we need first to consider the garden as a vehicle of *meaning*.

Or, better, a vehicle of several modes of meaning. Almost from the beginning of the Chinese tradition, gardens have been invested with representational functions. Around 100 BCE, the park created by the Han Emperor Wudi represented the mountain and island abodes of the Immortals, apparently in order to entice them to visit the park. Later gardens, often through the placing of rocks and pools, represented famous natural scenic areas. But the references of the Chinese garden could also be of a less tangible kind. Particular flowers came to be seen as expressive of moral qualities – chrysanthemums of simplicity, for example. And the informal, flowing contours of gardens in the Daoist style were held to express the quality of *wu wei*. The natural *look* of the garden was consonant with the naturalness or spontaneity of 'non-action'.

Chinese authors were alert, incidentally, to several senses of the term 'natural' in relation to gardens. A discussion in the eighteenth-century novel *Dream of the Red Chamber*, comparable to simultaneous debates being conducted in Europe, suggests for instance that 'natural' cannot always be the opposite of 'artificial', since craft may have gone into making a garden that is reasonably described as natural. This implies, rightly, that a simplistic opposition of nature and culture – the sort those outraged students were drawing – needs replacing by more nuanced distinctions.

It is when we turn to a further mode of meaning that we appreciate why, for Daoists, the garden challenges a stark opposition of nature and culture, and why the garden is of great significance for them. It is because of the ways in which culture and nature cooperate in the garden that it exemplifies and symbolises a wider co-dependence of human creative activity and the natural world as it is experienced. The meaning of the Daoist garden is a truth – which the garden itself embodies – about the relationship of nature and culture.

There are obvious physical ways in which the interventions of the gardener and natural phenomena affect one another. The fence the gardener erects protects the growth of plants; bad weather constrains what he or she can do. The bird table attracts more birds to the vicinity; moles ruin a new parterre. But interdependence takes the form, too, of reciprocal effects on experience. Consider the choice and placing of stones, which is an important aspect of Chinese and Japanese gardening.

The placing of a stone may be in response, as the Japanese put it, to 'the request of the stone' – to what is intimated after close, patient observation of the stone. Where it is placed may, in turn, render salient, otherwise inconspicuous, features of the surrounding landscape, perhaps 'borrowing' it as scenery. Or, as in many Italian gardens, the symmetrical layout of stones may exaggerate the perceived 'wildness' of the terrain beyond the garden. Conversely, the stones may have been placed so as to form protection for wild creatures whose existence is perceived, in our ecologically sensitive age, to be under threat.

One could go on, but the point is made that, in gardening, such is the scale and variety of co-dependence between human intervention and experience of the natural world, that the garden exemplifies (and is an apt symbol of) a general co-dependence between the human and the natural. This is the co-dependence spoken of in Chapter 6 in connection with Daoism's rejection of a dualism of selves and world, and again in Chapter 10 regarding the mutual dependence of human engagement and environments as spheres of significance. A sense of this co-dependence is a condition of a genuinely convergent relationship with nature.

The garden as an epitome of co-dependence resonates with the Daoist image of human beings supporting "the myriad things in their natural condition" or "nourishing" them (D 64, Z 33). This resonance is brought out by a contemporary author when he writes of Daoists as "gardeners of the cosmos . . . who slowly shape their life and environment", but also "let . . . nature take its course".[17] It is through human engagement that experience of the world assumes structure, that in effect there is a world to experience at all. At the same time, all engagement responds to ways of experiencing nature which are already there. This is what mindful gardeners, in their own small but significant domain, know. They see in the garden their own creations, but creations which, they know, are in turn responses to their experiences of the natural world.[18]

The co-dependence of nature and culture goes all the way back and all the way down. There is no cultural intervention and no experience of nature that is not shaped by a context, a form of life, that is itself a coming together of nature and culture. In the language of the *Zhuangzi*, there is no way of finally telling apart what is done by heaven (nature) and what is done by the human, so that "neither Heaven nor man is victor over the other" (Z 6). The doings of man and the processes of nature belong inseparably to that continual upsurge of experience – that coming to presence of a world – which is *dao*.

This is what the sage recognises, and it is why the mindful gardener is a candidate for sagehood. It is why, as suggested in the last chapter, the gardener's experience, more perhaps than 'the wilderness experience', is 'on the Way'.

Intervening for nature?

Yesterday morning, with summer giving way to autumn, I went to catch a last look at some favourite beech trees before their green changes to auburn. I had other options, of course. It was open to me, as to anyone, to join some 'eco-warriors' on their way to the Edinburgh Festival to protest against carbon emissions. Or I could have stayed at my desk and fired off an angry letter to a newspaper about the latest threat to a rare species of bird.

These would have been not just interventions in nature but, in aim at least, for the sake of nature. These days many people intervene in nature with the purpose of opposing, reversing or remedying 'industrial' interventions of the kind discussed in the previous chapter. These 'eco-interventionists' are activists committed to such goals as conservation, carbon-emission reduction, and opposition to logging or drilling.

My question is whether activist intervention on behalf of nature has to be a significant component, from a Daoist perspective, of an appropriate relationship to the natural world, and hence in a good human life. The answer might seem obvious. In this book, after all, we have encountered perverse ways in which human beings have treated natural environments and the creatures who belong there. So what could be more imperative than interventions designed to remedy those ways?

Activism and virtue

But this seems obvious only from the viewpoint of a distinctively modern conception of moral life – one briefly described in the opening chapter of this book. This conception combines two thoughts: I should determine what I do by considering what it would be good for people in general to do, and what is good for them to do is to produce certain practical results – increased welfare, reduced suffering, an improved environment, or whatever. The combined thought, therefore, is that I live rightly when I do things which, if done by people in general, have desirable practical outcomes.[1]

This approach is well entrenched in the literature of environmental ethics and policy. The moral task is often taken to be the establishment of principles which, if generally followed, would result in a better natural environment – in 'saving the planet', as the contemporary rhetoric has it. "We must make the rescue of the environment", declares Al Gore, "the central organizing principle for civilisation."[2]

This approach is sometimes found, too, in modern nature writing, where there is a discernible shift from 'I' to 'we' – from description of an author's personal relationship with the natural world to calls, like Gore's, for 'us' to take action on behalf of nature. But some of these authors appreciate too the importance for a person of 'nurturing' a close relationship to nature "without any need to feel that what you are doing is of any use".[3] Being in such a relationship is, quite simply, 'a better way to live'. The focus in a book by Richard Mabey, which sensitively describes the author's recovery from depression, is on "regaining [an] imaginative relationship with the [natural] world beyond" – for it is in this that he will find a "nature cure", a recovery of a "sensual engagement with the world, [a] link between feeling and intelligence", and an appreciation of "the inseparability of nature and culture".[4]

Some readers may respond that nurturing a closer or more imaginative relationship to nature is fine, but remains a merely personal, self-absorbed, even selfish ambition unless converted into active commitment to 'rescuing the environment'. These would be readers unconvinced by earlier chapters where, in the figure of the virtuous Daoist, we encountered an example – an exemplar, even – of the ethical life. The sage's life is one of self-cultivation informed by reflection on the good life – reflection which yields an understanding of the virtues conducive to a life that goes well. Daoist reflection considers how a life might best accord with *dao* and hence manifest *de*. It is a style of reflection which endorses mindfulness, humility, impartiality, respect for the integrity of creatures and appreciation of beauty. In turn, this attunement to the natural world informs the sage's comportment towards nature: a range of engagements and interventions consistent with *de*. The sage will not, for example, be found working on a factory farm or shooting turtle doves for fun.

Except by those in the grip of the modern picture, it won't be denied that the sage's life is an ethical one. That it is not a model which everyone might follow is beside the point. As is the fact that – for all that we have so far heard – the sage is not an environmental activist or eco-warrior. To deny, on these grounds, that the sage's life is an ethical one would indicate how parochial, yet entrenched, is the modern conception of morality. The same parochial conception would be to blame for the feeling that, without a call to activist engagement, the Daoist moral message lacks a radical edge. In its call for a transformation of the self – of the selves, at any rate, that most of us have become in modernity – Daoism surely shows its concern for the very roots of human existence.

Entrenchment of the modern conception helps explain one commentator's judgement that the classical Daoist texts are not "relevant to an environmental ethic".[5] Being concerned with "a high level of spiritual attainment" – even "mystical realisation" – means, he writes, that the texts cannot be "the basis of an environmental ethic applicable to everyone". For a person's relationship to the natural world to be an ethical one, he implies, it must aim at practical outcomes of a sort to which everyone could commit. This idea that the goal of 'spiritual attainment' counts *against* the ethical complexion of a person's concerns would have surprised the authors of the Daoist texts – as it would their Greek and Indian contemporaries. For, among these thinkers, it was precisely this goal – self-cultivation, self-transformation – that distinguished the ethical life.

A reasonable question to raise, though, is this: granted the primacy Daoism gives to self-cultivation, why shouldn't this involve environmentalist commitments? Might it not be that self-cultivation is possible only through actively exercising such commitments? And the question might be accompanied by the claim that, at least in Daoist religious tradition, there is indeed evidence of interventionism.

Mention may be made here of the second- or third-century CE *One Hundred and Eighty Precepts* (*Yibaibashijie*) of The Way of the Celestial Masters, a main tendency in organised Daoist religion. Around 20 Precepts forbid improper treatment of natural creatures and environments – wantonly felling trees, disturbing birds, contaminating lakes and rivers, and so on. But, while the Precepts display a prescient ecological awareness, their primary point, it seems, was to instruct 'libationers' – leaders of religious communities – on the respectful maintenance of sacred spaces and refuges from the 'dust and grime' of the everyday world. As such, the Precepts were not intended to formulate an environmentalist public policy, but to ensure felicitous conditions for adepts to develop their personal relationship to *dao*.[6]

A similar point might be made about many Daoist declarations on the environment made over the last few decades.[7] While these borrow from the rhetoric of both Western environmentalism and religious ecumenicalism, the emphasis is generally not on the rescue of the global environment but on the protection of local environments – those of temples, especially – which have particular spiritual significance.

It is true that various recent declarations include references to Laozi as 'the God of ecology' and to *dao* as a 'Grandmother Goddess' who 'came to Earth to enlighten humanity', but it would be rash to assume much affinity between contemporary Daoist religiosity and the philosophy of the classic texts, which has been the focus in this book. For there is nothing in these texts to support such references. So even if the declarations express a more muscular environmentalism than I have suggested is to be found within Daoism, little could be inferred as to the line taken in the *Daodejing* and the *Zhuangzi*.

Let's now consider this line – undogmatically and conscious of how different our contemporary situation is from the context in which the classic Daoist texts were composed.

Environmentalism and *wu wei*

"The attitudes and values consistent with modern environmentalism should not be sought in the 'classical' texts," writes a distinguished student of Daoism.[8] What might warrant his judgement?

To begin with, absent from these texts are several ingredients in Western environmental ethics that help to fuel today's ecological activism. There is no notion, for example, of the *rights* of nature or of future generations: hence, no concept of a *violation* of rights that only robust intervention can remedy. Indeed, the texts (D 81, for example) speak against the strident moralising exemplified by the rhetoric of rights.

Nor, probably, would their authors have sympathy for the fashionable idea of human beings as 'stewards of nature'. No god has appointed human beings to look after the earth, and it inflates their importance to suppose that they can "seriously and permanently 'derail' nature"[9] and then put it back on track. Those words are Stephen Jay Gould's, who adds – more contentiously – that "on geological scales, our planet will take good care of itself" and "clear the impact of any human malfeasance". For Daoists, the stewardship image may betray the same hubris as the industrial interventions in nature against which stewardship is supposed to be the antidote.

The stewardship image is encouraged, in part, by a vision of an ecological crisis or disaster from which the environment needs to be rescued. We stewards, it seems, must also be saviours of the planet. The response to this vision by the founder of Orthodox Daoism of America was to remark "I see no crisis" and to accuse those who speak of "crisis and cure" of encouraging an "aggressive" interventionism at odds with a calm, Daoist acceptance that "things change".[10] Zhuangzi would perhaps agree, and add the important observation that the perception of crisis or catastrophe is a perspectival one. For whom exactly is global warming, say, a disaster? Certainly there will be people and animals – from Bangladesh to the Arctic Circle – whose existence it threatens. But there are also countless insects and marine creatures, and some people, who will prosper from it. Considered impartially, the claim goes, there is simply change, not crisis or disaster.

That's a claim which some will challenge.[11] They will argue that, despite Gould's opinion, human intervention in nature has been so gross and decisive as to have derailed the natural world, which has thereby fallen out of harmony with *dao*. This resulting disharmony is not just 'change', and perception of it as a disaster is not merely perspectival. To this, the Orthodox Daoist just cited might not unreasonably reply that, while the modern world has indeed been shaped by people who have lost the Way, this world can't itself be described as being no longer 'on the Way'. It's not as if human intervention has suspended the laws of nature through which *dao* holds sway over everything.

There is another idea which, for a similar reason, may have no appeal for Daoists, despite playing a central role in modern environmental ethics. This is the idea of nature's 'intrinsic value'. As Zhuangzi, like Nietzsche, recognised, the values we ascribe to the natural world are discernible only to creatures like ourselves, with our kind of interests. From the fish's or the mosquito's perspective, what we deem useful or beautiful may be destructive or ugly. Perspectivism precludes the notion of values that are there in the world independently of any creature's perspective. Zhuangzi would also note the irony in a notion which – supposedly invoked to counter humanity's disdain for nature – ignores all "views of right and wrong" except human ones. How could a person be more "arrogantly separated . . . off from the creatures of the world" (Z 33)?

Rejection of talk of an ecological crisis and of nature's intrinsic value is encouraged, then, by Daoist perspectivism. There is no perspective-free 'view from nowhere' from which to validate such talk. But Daoists do not reject what Gould calls a 'legitimately parochial interest' in the lives and fates of human beings and the creatures that exist alongside us. The Daoist sage, we saw, is not a cold fish: he enjoys the beauties of nature and the company of friends, and is saddened by the illness of a colleague or, as Liezi's remarks on animals imply, by the death of a pig or a bird (L 2). Such pleasures and sorrows reflect 'parochial', but 'legitimate', concerns. The sage does not pretend that these are feelings that all creatures must experience, but they are the natural, spontaneous responses of men and women liberated from the dominion of ambitions and prejudices. As responses that do not contend with, or impose upon, other beings, they accord with the virtue of *wu wei*.

The question arises, then, whether environmental activism isn't mandatory in the light of legitimate, though admittedly parochial (or perspectival), concerns and hopes. If it is appropriate for me to be worried by the declining number of greenfinches, is it not incumbent on me to help remedy the situation?

It would be too quick for a Daoist, by way of a negative response, simply to invoke the idea of *wu wei*. For, as we've noted, this is not intended as a blanket rejection of action. Though there certainly are remarks in the *Daodejing*, elaborating on *wu wei*, which discourage engagement in large-scale, muscular and morally strident interventions, and which instead urge an 'enlightened self-restraint'. Sages "do not contend" and "never strive for the great" (D 66, 63); they "prefer tranquillity" and allow people to "regulate themselves" (D 57). They act in the spirit of the wise ruler for whom "governing a great state is like cooking a small fish" (D 60) – something to be done gently, with minimal interference.

The reason why Daoists might be reluctant environmental activists is not, as is sometimes suggested, that they consider the world to be governed by an entirely benign power – so that interference with it, even for remedial purposes, can only be misguided. *Dao* is too impersonal to be described as benign, and it is expressly denied that heaven and earth are "humane" or "benevolent" (D 5). The reason, rather, is that activist commitment can involve illusion or pretence.

Such a commitment, for a start, requires belief in the merits of long-term planning, in defiance of Zhuangzi's advice to remain pliant, to avoid becoming "a repository of plans and schemes" (Z 7). Nor could a Daoist pretend to have the certainty about the effects of interventions that is necessary to engaging in them with confidence. Indeed, the evidence of destructive technological interventions – some of them made with good intentions – is that 'great undertakings' easily misfire. People who profess knowledge of future outcomes only appear to be following the Way and are in fact on the way to ignorance (D 38).

Responsible Daoists will heed Zhuangzi's cautionary tale of two well-meaning emperors who repay the generosity of a third, but physically limited, emperor by drilling holes in him so that he may "see, hear, eat and breathe". On the seventh day, he dies (Z 7). (This tale has a larger lesson to teach, for the unfortunate emperor, Hundun, is the personification of the 'chaos', or 'unhewn' condition that precedes the division of the world into discrete objects. The anecdote is a warning against a "calculating skill" that is destructive of "heavenly genuineness".[12])

One reason, for the Daoist, why there can be little confidence in ambitious planning is that nature – while obeying certain general rhythms – is volatile. "Time cannot be stopped", observes Zhuangzi: nature is forever:

> ... waxing and waning, filling and emptying, each end is succeeded by a new beginning ... the becoming of things is like a galloping horse, transforming with each moment. (Z 17)

Attempting to conserve an animal or plant species, for instance, far from being an intervention on behalf of nature, may be an artificial and fruitless effort to defy nature's transformative character.

Note, too, that human perspectives are also subject to transformation. "You [too] will in any case be spontaneously transforming", Zhuangzi reminds us (Z 17). Who can tell, therefore, whether the predilections that direct today's environmentalist strategies will be shared by those who eventually inherit the effects of these strategies? Would people alive today enjoy the sort of world that their medieval Christian ancestors tried to bequeath?

As these remarks suggest, environmental activism can be guilty of disguising the partiality of the perspectives that inspire it – a partiality in excess of 'legitimately parochial' concern. "The *dao* of heaven has no preferences, no favourites" (D 79). We human agents can't fully emulate the *dao* in this respect, but that is no reason to excuse the favouritism that inspires many ecological policies. Red squirrels and grey squirrels; whales and salmon; wooded valleys and stretches of tundra. It is hard to understand, even from a 'legitimately parochial' standpoint, why only the fate of the first in each of these pairs matters to most people.

There are two more 'pretences' of some environmental activists which the Daoist discerns. Both are connected with the matter of effectiveness. The first and more crucial is the pretence that natural environments can be rescued from degradation without a suspension or thorough transformation of the current lifestyle of people in developed, and indeed developing, countries. It ought to be apparent that where conflict arises between environmentalist interventions and the imperatives of economic growth and ever-rising standards of living, there is no real contest. Only in a world – very different from our actual one – shaped by ideals of frugality, simplicity and self-restraint could 'rescuing the environment' seriously compete with ambitions of a more materialist kind.

Maybe that's too gloomy. Or maybe not gloomy enough – if Daoist reservations about nature itself being 'in crisis' are misplaced. But, either way, there is a second 'pretence' in which many people indulge, for they often exaggerate the likely significance of their individual contributions to environmentalist causes. Honest recognition of the very limited nature of one's own contribution prompts reflection on the place that activist commitment should have in one's life. Those who understand the essentials of life, remarks Zhuangzi, "do not labour themselves over the aspects of life that deliberate activity can do nothing about" (Z 19). "But what", somebody will protest, "if everyone thought like that!?" Well, this is a protest that only someone who is committed to our modern conception of morality would make. For those, Daoists included, who embrace a conception of ethics as cultivation of virtue – of excellence of character – it is not a cogent objection.

Daoism and quietism

The thrust of the preceding section was that, for the Daoist, it may not be through environmental activism that an individual best engages in the task of self-cultivation, of aspiring to live well. Radical self-transformation does not entail radical politics. The guiding thought, it seems, is that activism ties one too closely to a kind of world from which the Daoist, in a spirit of quietism, seeks to disengage.

But is the label of 'quietism' really an apt one? A good reason for rejecting it, some would say, is that in the *Daodejing* part of the case for *wu wei* is the Machiavellian one that through reticence and seeming to yield, a person achieves his or her goals; political and economic ones included. (Hence the popularity of books on how Daoism can make you a successful businessman, soldier or administrator.) A person who "conducts affairs on the principle of *wu wei*" brings "everything into order" (D 3), and *wu wei* has the same advantage as that "softest thing in the world", water, since it penetrates and overcomes everything else (D 43). The advice, it seems, is not to be quietistic, but only to pretend to be.

The importance of these remarks has, however, been exaggerated. The *Daodejing* is an eclectic work, in which the Machiavellian strand is only one among several. Moreover, the Machiavellian advice is addressed specifically to political rulers who, the idea goes, govern better when they give the appearance of governing less. It is a mistake to suppose that, even in the *Daodejing*, the advice to dissimulate in order to succeed is intended for the conduct of life in general. And in other Daoist works, such as the *Neiye* and the *Zhuangzi*, this strand is barely discernible. Laozi's comparison of the effectiveness of reticent, low-profile behaviour to water is not repeated by Zhuangzi, who instead uses the water metaphor to illuminate points about knowledge and spontaneity. And for him, the "usefulness of uselessness" resides not in achievements by someone who pretends to be ineffective but, as with a tree having no commercial use, in the protection and growth of people who keep their distance from the business of everyday practical life (Z 4). While activity of some kind cannot be avoided, the sage "lets go of the world", thereby becoming "free of entanglements" (Z 19).

If this is quietism, it is not, however, the quietism of indifference. Daoism teaches concern with and regret for human beings' treatment of natural environments and the creatures which live in them. Daoist sages are persons of compassion, not out of commitment to a moral principle enjoining the maximisation of utility, but because – released from a sharp sense of personal identity that separates individuals – care for oneself naturally carries over into care for other beings. This is why one of Laozi's 'three treasures', alongside frugality and uncompetitive humility, is kindness or compassion (D 67).

Nor is it quietism in a fatalistic tone, like the one heard in some of the verses of *The Book of Odes*. Why, these verses ask, should we care about the wider world given the impossibility of escaping the inevitable routine of our lives – getting up and going to bed, digging and tilling, drinking and eating? Rather, it is the quietism (if we persist with the label) of people for whom a mode of self-cultivation has primacy.

For the Daoist, the world of everyday human business is 'too much with us', so that the task is to secure a personal moral space on the edge of this world. It is "sham virtue", says Zhuangzi, to "produce regulations [and] standards" for humankind, and the sage's concern should not be to "rule anything outside himself" (Z 7). This does not mean the sage has to be a hermit or dropout. He may be quietly and without ostentation moving among us, getting on with life. While the moral space secured is personal, moreover, this does not mean it is private and exclusively 'inner'. Cultivation, as we saw in Chapter 10, is as much 'bio' as 'spiritual', no less a discipline of the body than of the soul. Or, better, it is cultivation of a person or self which, being nothing more than an experiential route through the world, cannot be divided up into separate components.

The Daoist contribution

It is because self-cultivation is not focused on the 'inner' rather than the 'outer' that it requires an appropriate attunement and comportment towards the natural world. Engagements with nature of the kinds described in earlier chapters help to secure the moral space – the arena in which to develop virtue – which Daoists hope to occupy. This is why the metaphor of Daoists as gardeners of the world – as cultivators of personal landscapes – is an apt one.

While Daoists engage with natural environments, their engagement is also a retreat – not from an 'outer' to an 'inner' world, but from a frenzied world of activity and ambition to a quieter haven. From this haven, they have no illusions about 'saving the planet'. Like one distinguished nature writer, they eschew "plans for reorganisation and reconstruction". But, also like him, they will want "to reduce somewhat the level of suffering where [they] encountered it"[13] and, more generally, to serve in small, local and undramatic ways to protect and enhance the natural environments with which they engage. In doing so, they live naturally or spontaneously, for their actions are not dictated by principles and plans, but are mindful and pliant responses to the situations and contexts they encounter.

Daoists, then, are unlikely to be found among 'eco-warriors', but they will be found tending gardens, feeding birds in winter, protecting local wildlife from clumsy combine harvesters, opposing plans for a factory farm near their villages, and encouraging their neighbours to appreciate the useful uselessness of a threatened grove of trees. If this sounds insufficiently radical, one should recall that it is a way of living that is achieved only through a deep transformation of the self.

The theme of this book has been convergence with the natural world. Convergence is not a single accomplishment – the acceptance of a big statement about people and nature, or a heroic commitment on behalf of nature. Convergence is what Daoist sages exemplify in their attunement to and comportment towards nature – their complex of moods, understanding, appreciation, pleasures, engagements and interventions. Daoism's contribution to environmental ethics is not a new principle for governing humankind's treatment of the environment, nor a new plan for rescuing the planet. It is, instead, a portrait of how an individual person, in seeking consonance with the source of things – with *dao* – may live well in relation to nature.

Notes

Chapter 1

1 Writers on nature whom I have enjoyed, learned from, and cite in the course of this book include Richard Mabey, Robert Macfarlane, Roger Deakin, Simon Barnes, Annie Dillard, Michael Pollan, Barry Lopez and Mark Cocker.

2 Pollan, p.206.

3 Mabey 2006, p.207.

4 Macfarlane 2004

5 See Annas, Ch 1.

6 Baker, pp.10, 48, 95, 121, 145.

7 Thoreau 1999, p.282.

8 Lopez, pp.83, 124.

9 Lawrence, p.284.

10 'Gain's Law'. Hodgson 2003, p.34.

11 In Cotter, p.321.

12 Dillard, pp.9, 66, 170.

13 de Waal, p.301.

14 See James, *The Presence of Nature*, a book with whose judgements many of my own correspond.

15 See, especially, Hadot.

Chapter 2

1 For Zong Bing's essay, see de Bary, pp.253–4.

2 'Returning to Live in the Country (I)' and 'Autumn Chrysanthemums of Beautiful Colour'. Tao Qian's poems can be accessed at http://personaltao.com/gallery/poetry/poetry-of-tao-qian.

3 Yutang, p.112.

4 See Ames and Rosemont, p.150.

5 Fung, p.31.

6 See Kirkland 2004, p.33.

Chapter 3

1   See White for an influential statement of the view discussed in this section.
2   See his essay 'Evolution and ethics', p.83.
3   Quoted in Trilling, pp.129–30.
4   See Hunt and Willis on Walpole's and similar attitudes.
5   See Sharr, pp.64–5.
6   Heidegger's views on technology are articulated in several of the essays in Heidegger 1975 and 1977.
7   Heidegger's reference to the *dao* is in his essay 'The nature of language' (in Heidegger 1971, p.92).
8   On Heidegger's debt to Daoism and the translation project, see May.
9   Guo Xiang (252–312 CE) also edited the work and may have written parts of it too. Selections from his commentary are in Ziporyn's translation of the *Zhuangzi*.
10   'Following what is spontaneous' and 'taking no action that is contrary to nature' – these characterisations are by, respectively, Wang Bi (the third-century CE editor of the *Daodejing*) and the twentieth-century philosopher Wing-tsit Chan, and are cited by Wang Keping in his translation of the *Daodejing*.

Chapter 4

1   Woolfson, p.102.
2   Fowles, pp.138–40.
3   'Snow', Hodgson 2008, p.98.
4   Barnes, p.216.
5   Macfarlane 2007, p.157.
6   Murdoch, p.378.
7   James, §5.2

Chapter 5

1   LaChapelle, p.90.
2   On Chinese terms translatable by 'nature', see Hahn.
3   On the *Taiping jing*, see Kohn 1993, pp.191ff, and Lai.
4   On the *bajing* sites, see Li.
5   Macfarlane 2007, p.32.
6   Ibid., pp.234, 316.
7   See Allan.
8   See Graham 1989, especially Part IV.

9   In Gill, 'The Tables Turned', p.131.
10   Cited in Li, p.152.
11   Macfarlane 2007, p.100.
12   In Gill, p.270.
13   Ortega y Gasset, p.114.
14   Wang Wei (eighth century), in Harris, p.224.
15   The Preface to the Orchid Pavilion poems may be accessed at
     http://en.wikisource.org/wiki/Preface_to_the_Poems_Composed_at_
     the_Orchid_Pavilion.

Chapter 6

1   I have in mind Lionel Giles' 1912 translation of the *Liezi* and Arthur
     Waley's 1934 translation of the *Daodejing*.
2   Kohn 2009, p.23.
3   Zhang Songru, cited by Wang Keping in his translation of the *Daodejing*,
     p.24.
4   Hanfeizi in Chan, p.260.
5   Guo Xiang, in Ziporyn, p.139.
6   On Zhuangzi and language as a useful communicative tool, see Hansen.
7   Wittgenstein, §38.
8   Heidegger 1971, p.92.
9   Moeller, p.147.
10   On the significance of wheel and jar metaphors, see Moeller.
11   In Chan, p.323.

Chapter 7

1   For the passage from *The Doctrine of the Mean*, see Chan, pp.107ff.
2   Fung, p.100.
3   A concept developed by Fox, especially pp.53ff.
4   See Hall and Ames.
5   Guo Xiang in Ziporyn, p.208.
6   In my sketch of the sage I use the masculine pronoun, not because there
     cannot be women sages, but because the figures in the ancient poems, texts
     and paintings that inspire the sketch are all men.
7   My remarks on spontaneity owe much to A. C. Graham's introduction to
     his translation of the *Zhuangzi*, especially p.14.
8   The phrase is from Schopenhauer, Vol I, p.99.

Chapter 8

1   For these and other texts recording the 'preoccupations' of 'religious' Daoism, see Kohn 1993.

2   The Digha Nikaya ('Long Discourses'), Sutta 22.

3   In Gill, p.270.

4   Ziporyn, p.247.

5   Cited in Mabey 2005, p.148.

6   Dillard, pp.21, 34, 80.

7   Mabey 2005, p.148.

8   A. C. Graham's comment in his translation of the *Zhuangzi*, p.107.

9   For Ge Hong's *Baopuzi* ('Book of the Master Who Embraces Simplicity'), see Kohn 1993, especially pp.197ff and pp.306ff.

10   For selections from the *Huainanzi*, see Chan, pp.305–8.

11   Ziporyn p.132.

12   Bachelard 1994, pp.xvi, 184.

13   Rousseau, p.94f.

14   Rousseau, p.91.

15   Rousseau, p.12.

16   Bachelard 1971, p.167.

17   Rousseau, p.92.

18   Bachelard 1971, p.175.

19   Bachelard 1994, p.102.

20   Tao Qian's poems can be accessed at http://personaltao.com/gallery/poetry/poetry-of-tao-qian.

21   Bachelard 1971, p.173.

22   On Buddhism and mindfulness, see Nyanaponika, pp.102, 108. He describes a mindfulness that approximates to reverie, a 'pliancy of mind' enabling a person to experience things, not in their 'artificial isolation', but in relation to their past, environment, context and 'wider pattern'. See, too, the discussion in James, §4.2, on 'selfless attention', which also draws on Nyanaponika's authority.

Chapter 9

1   'Reading the Classic of the Hills and Seas'. Tao Qian's poems can be accessed at http://personaltao.com/gallery/poetry/poetry-of-tao-qian.

2   In Harris, p.191.

3   Deakin, p.155.

4   Bernhard, p. 62.

5   Cocker, p.109.

6   Barnes, p.237.

7   Schopenhauer, Vol II, p.354.

8   Michel Houellebecq, cited in James, p.67.

9   Balcombe, p.22.

10   On criticisms of aesthetic appreciation of nature, see Brady.

11   On Chinese terms translatable by 'beautiful' and 'good', see Wang Keping's discussion in his translation of the *Daodejing*, pp.106–7.

12   Emerson, p.4.

13   On the relationship between beauty and virtue, see Cooper 2010.

14   In Harris, p.217.

Chapter 10

1   In Harris, p.117.

2   In Harris, p.235.

3   In Harris, p.191.

4   Deakin, p.283.

5   See Heidegger 1971, especially 'The Thing'.

6   Lopez, p.117.

7   Macfarlane 2007, p.203.

8   Morpurgo, pp.112ff.

9   In Harris, p.97.

10   Kirkland 2004, p.33.

11   Schipper 1993, p.xiv.

12   Wittgenstein, p.178^{e}.

13   Schipper 1993, p.214.

14   Zhuang and Wang, p. 355

15   Schipper 1993, p.139.

16   Schipper 1993, p.138.

17   For the *Daoyin tu* and related documents on bodily exercise, see Kohn 1993, pp.141–8.

18   Harmony between a person's 'inner' world and 'outer' reality – between 'interior' and 'exterior' landscapes – is a familiar theme in modern nature writing. See, for example, Macfarlane 2007, p.24, and Lopez, p.9.

Chapter 11

1   Thoreau 1993, pp.108ff.

2   Petrarch, p.44.

3   Barnes, pp.158, 165, 282.

4   A. C. Graham's comment in his translation of the *Zhuangzi*, p.14.

5   Wang Keping in his translation of the *Daodejing*, p.205.

6   Ortega y Gasset, quoted in Pollan, p.343.
7   www.cic-wildlife.org/index.php?id=16.
8   In Pollan, p.336.
9   Quoted in Keswick, p.33.
10   In Pollan, p.343.
11   Raffel, pp.44, 159, 205.
12   Baker, pp.10, 14.

Chapter 12

1   W. S. Blunt, quoted in Passmore, pp.180–1
2   Ian McHarg, quoted in Passmore, pp.180–1.
3   Locke, §32 and §34.
4   Spengler's *Man and Technics* as cited in Cooper 1999.
5   Ernst Jünger *(Der Arbeiter)* as cited in Cooper 1999.
6   On Meng Tian's 'crime', see Parkes, pp.198–9.
7   Yanagi, pp.215, 224; see also p.108.
8   Mencius' remarks on farming are mainly in III A:3 of his book (see Lau).
9   On ancient Chinese agriculture, see Anderson.
10   On 'the Agricultural school' and the 'Spring and Autumn Annals', see Fung, Chs 2 & 3.
11   See Bonsdorff.
12   Powers, pp. 99f.
13   Giono, p.413.
14   Marx, p.140.
15   The story of the outraged students is told in LaFargue, p.47.
16   On the *Yuan Ye* and Chinese gardens generally, see Keswick and Wang.
17   Miller, p.46.
18   On Daoism and the significance of gardens, see also Meyer, LaFargue and Cooper 2006, especially Ch. 7.

Chapter 13

1   Philosophers will notice that the sketch of this 'distinctively modern conception' of morality combines two traditions – Kantian and 'consequentialist' – usually contrasted with one another.
2   Gore as cited in Johnstone, p.9.
3   Barnes, pp.281–2.
4   Mabey 2005, pp.50, 64.
5   Meyer, pp.231–2.

6   On the *One Hundred and Eighty Precepts*, see Kohn 1993, pp.97ff, and
      Schipper 2001.
7   Several recent Daoist declarations on the environment and ecology are
      published on the ARC (Alliance of Religions and Conservation) website,
      see, for example, www.arcworld.org/faiths.asp?pageID=11.
8   Kirkland 2001, p.283.
9   Gould, p.314.
10   Liu Ming (aka Charles Belyea), in Girardot et al., pp.379ff.
11   Graham Parkes robustly challenges this claim in correspondence with me.
12   Shi Deqing, cited in Ziporyn, p.212. Graham Parkes pointed out to me the
      need to mention this larger moral of the cautionary tale.
13   Lopez, p.123.

Bibliography

Daoist philosophical texts

The *Daodejing*

I have consulted several translations of this work, but have relied primarily on:

Philip J. Ivanhoe (2002) *The Daodejing of Laozi.* Indianapolis: Hackett Publishing Company.

Wang Keping (1998) *The Classic of the Dao: A new investigation.* Beijing: Foreign Languages Press. (There is now a revised edition of this work, titled *Reading the Dao: A thematic inquiry.* London: Continuum, 2010.)

The Book of *Zhuangzi*

Again, I have drawn on several translations, but have mainly relied on:

A. C. Graham (2001) *Chuang-Tzu: The inner chapters.* Indianapolis: Hackett Publishing Company.

Brook Ziporyn (2009) *Zhuangzi: The Essential Writings, with Selections from Traditional Commentaries.* Indianapolis: Hackett Publishing Company.

For Guo Xiang's Commentary on the *Zhuangzi* I have used the selections from Ziporyn's book.

The Book of *Liezi*

I have relied on:

A. C. Graham (1990) *The Book of Lieh-Tzu: A classic of Tao.* New York: Columbia University Press.

The *Neiye*

I have used the translation by Harold Roth at www.stillness.com/tao/neiyeh.txt.

Other works cited

Allan, Sarah (1997) *The Way of Water and Sprouts of Virtue.* Albany: State University of New York Press.

Ames, Roger T. (2001) 'Putting the *Te* back into Taoism', in Callicott and Ames (eds), *Nature in Asian Traditions of Thought: Essays in Environmental Philosophy.* Albany: State University of New York Press, pp.113–44.

Ames, Roger T. and Rosemont, Henry (trs) (1998) *The Analects of Confucius: A philosophical translation.* New York: Ballantine Books.

Anderson, E. N. (1988) *The Food of China*. New Haven: Yale University Press.

Annas, Julia (1993) *The Morality of Happiness*. Oxford: Oxford University Press.

Armstrong, Susan and Botzler, Richard (eds) (1993) *Environmental Ethics: Divergence and convergence*. New York: McGraw-Hill.

Bachelard, Gaston, *The Poetics of Reverie*, tr. D. Russell (1971). Boston: Beacon Press.

Bachelard, Gaston, *The Poetics of Space*, tr. M. Jolas (1994). Boston: Beacon Press.

Baker, J. A. (2005 edn) *The Peregrine*. New York: New York Review of Books.

Balcombe, Jonathan (2007) *Pleasurable Kingdom: Animals and the nature of feeling good*. London: Macmillan.

Barnes, Simon (2007) *How To Be Wild*. London: Short Books.

Bary, William T. de; Watson, Burton and Chan, Wing-tsit (eds) (1960) *Sources of Chinese Tradition* Vol I. New York: Columbia University Press.

Bernhard, Thomas (1992 edn), *Wittgenstein's Nephew: A friendship*, tr. E. Osers. London: Vintage.

Bonsdorff, Pauline von (2008) 'Agriculture, aesthetic appreciation and the worlds of nature', in S. Arntzen and E. Brady (eds), *Humans in the Land. The ethics and aesthetics of the cultural landscape*. Oslo: Unipub, pp.159–76.

Brady, Emily (2003) *Aesthetics of the Natural Environment*. Edinburgh: Edinburgh University Press.

Callicott, J. B. and Ames, Roger T. (eds) (2001) *Nature in Asian Traditions of Thought: Essays in Environmental Philosophy*. Albany: State University of New York Press.

Chan, Wing-tsit (1969) *A Source Book in Chinese Philosophy*. Princeton: Princeton University Press.

Cocker, Mark (2007) *Crow Country*. London: Jonathan Cape.

Coetzee, J. M. (1999) *The Lives of Animals*. Princeton: Princeton University Press.

Cooper, David E. (1999) 'Reactionary Modernism', in Anthony O'Hear (ed.), *German Philosophy Since Kant*. Cambridge: Cambridge University Press, pp.291–304.

Cooper, David E. (2006) *A Philosophy of Gardens*. Oxford: Oxford University Press.

Cooper, David E. (2010) 'Edification and the experience of beauty', in Wang Keping (ed.), *Diversity and Unity in Aesthetics: International Yearbook of Aesthetics*, 14, pp.62–81.

Cotter, G. (ed.) (1988) *Natural History Verse: An anthology*. London: Christopher Helm Publishers.

Deakin, Roger (2009) *Notes from Walnut Tree Farm*. London: Penguin.

Dillard, Annie (2007 edn.) *Pilgrim at Tinker Creek*. New York: HarperCollins.

Emerson, Ralph Waldo. 'Nature (1844)', at www.bartleby.com/5/114.html.

Fowles, John (1993) 'Seeing nature whole', in Armstrong and Botzler (eds), *Environmental Ethics: Divergence and convergence*. New York: McGraw-Hill, pp.138–41.

Fox, Warwick (2006) *A Theory of General Ethics: Human relationships, nature and the built environment*. Cambridge, Massachusetts: MIT Press.

Fung, Yu-lan, *A Short History of Chinese Philosophy*, tr. D. Bodde (1966), New York: Free Press.

Gill, Stephen (ed.) (1984) *William Wordsworth: A Critical Edition of the Major Works*. Oxford: Oxford University Press.

Giono, Jean (1999 edn.) *Joy of Man's Desiring*, tr. Katherine Clarke. New York: Counterpoint Press.

Girardot, N. J.; Miller, James and Xiaogan, Liu (eds) (2001) *Daoism and Ecology: Ways within a cosmic landscape*. Cambridge, Massachusetts: Harvard University Press.

Gould, Stephen Jay (1993) 'The golden rule – a proper scale for our environmental crisis', in Armstrong and Botzler (eds), *Environmental Ethics: Divergence and convergence*. New York: McGraw-Hill, pp.310–15.

Graham, A. C. (1989) *Disputers of the Tao: Philosophical argument in Ancient China*. La Salle, Illinois: Open Court Publishing.

Hadot, Pierre (1995) *Philosophy as a Way of Life*, tr. M. Chase. Oxford: Blackwell.

Hahn, Thomas H. (2001) 'An introductory study on Daoist notions of wilderness', in Girardot et al. (eds) *Daoism and Ecology: Ways within a cosmic landscape*. Cambridge, Massachusetts: Harvard University Press, pp.201–18.

Hall, David L. (2001) 'On seeking a change of environment', in Callicott and Ames (eds) *Nature in Asian Traditions of Thought: Essays in Environmental Philosophy*. Albany: State University of New York Press, pp.99–112.

Hansen, Chad (1992) *A Daoist Theory of Chinese Thought: A philosophical interpretation*. Oxford: Oxford University Press.

Harris, Peter (tr. & ed.) (2009) *Three Hundred Tang Poems*. New York: Alfred A. Knopf.

Heidegger, Martin, *On the Way to Language*, tr. P. Hertz (1971), New York: Harper & Row.

Heidegger, Martin, *Poetry, Language, Thought*, tr. A. Hofstadter (1975). New York: Harper & Row.

Heidegger, Martin, *The Question Concerning Technology and Other Essays*, tr. W. Lovitt (1977). New York: Harper & Row.

Hodgson, Noel (2003) *Below Flodden*. Alnwick: Reiver Press.

Hodgson, Noel (2008) *Dancing Over Cheviot*, Cornhill: Reiver Press.

Hunt, John. D. and Willis, Peter (eds) (1988) *The Genius of the Place: The English Landscape Garden 1620–1820*. Cambridge, Massachusetts: MIT Press.

Huxley, T. H. (1894) *Collected Essays*. London: Macmillan.

James, Simon P. (2009) *The Presence of Nature: A study in Phenomenology and Environmental Philosophy*. Basingstoke: Palgrave Macmillan.

Johnstone, Ian M. 'Gatherings: Nature writing', http://ecopsychology.org/journal/ezine/naturewriting.html.

Keswick, Maggie (1980) *The Chinese Garden: History, Art and Architecture*, London: Academy.

Kirkland, Russell (2001) '"Responsible non-action" in a natural world',

in Girardot et al. (eds) *Daoism and Ecology: Ways within a cosmic landscape.*
Cambridge, Massachusetts: Harvard University Press, pp.283–304.

Kirkland, Russell (2004) *Taoism: The Enduring Tradition.* London: Routledge.

Kohn, Livia (2009) *Introducing Daoism.* London: Routledge.

Kohn, Livia (ed.) (1993) *The Taoist Experience: An anthology.* Albany: State
University of New York Press.

LaChapelle, Dolores (1988) *Sacred Land, Sacred Sex: Rapture of the Deep.*
Silverton, Colorado: Finn Hill Arts.

Lai, Chi-tim (2001) 'The Daoist concept of Central Harmony in the Scripture
of Great Peace: human responsibility for the maladies of nature', in Girardot
et al. (eds) *Daoism and Ecology: Ways within a cosmic landscape.* Cambridge,
Massachusetts: Harvard University Press, pp.95–111.

LaFargue, Michael (2001) '"Nature" as part of human culture in Daoism',
in Girardot et al. (eds), *Daoism and Ecology: Ways within a cosmic landscape.*
Cambridge, Massachusetts: Harvard University Press, pp.45–60.

Lau, D. C. (tr.) (1970) *Mencius.* London: Penguin.

Lawrence, D. H. (1994 edn.) *The Complete Poems.* Ware: Wordsworth Editions.

Li, Kairan (2009) *Landscape Improvement and Scenic Sites in Pre-modern China: A
critical review.* PhD thesis, University of Sheffield.

Locke, John (1967 edn.) *Two Treatises of Government.* Cambridge: Cambridge
University Press.

Lopez, Barry (2004) *Vintage Lopez.* New York: Vintage Books.

Mabey, Richard (2005) *Nature Cure.* London: Chatto & Windus.

Mabey, Richard (2006) *Gilbert White: A biography of the author of* The Natural
History of Selbourne. London: Profile Books.

Macfarlane, Robert (2004) *Mountains of the Mind: A History of a Fascination.*
London: Granta Books.

Macfarlane, Robert (2007) *The Wild Places.* London: Granta Books.

Marx, Karl (1979 edn.) *Early Texts*, ed. D. McLellan. Oxford: Blackwell.

May, Reinhard (1996) *Heidegger's Hidden Sources*, translated and with an
accompanying essay by Graham Parkes. London: Routledge.

Meyer, Jeffrey F. (2001) 'Salvation in the garden: Daoism and ecology', in
Girardot et al. (eds), *Daoism and Ecology: Ways within a cosmic landscape.*
Cambridge, Massachusetts: Harvard University Press, pp.219–36.

Miller, James (2003) *Daoism: A Short Introduction.* Oxford: Oneworld Publications.

Moeller, Hans-Georg (2004) *Daoism Explained.* Chicago: Open Court Publishing.

Morpurgo, Michael (2009) *Running Wild.* London: HarperCollins.

Murdoch, Iris (1997) *Existentialists and Mystics.* London: Penguin.

Nyanaponika (1994) *The Vision of Dhamma.* Kandy, Sri Lanka: Buddhist
Publication Society.

Ortega y Gasset, José (1962) *History as a System and Other Essays Toward a
Philosophy of History*, tr. H. Weyl. New York: W. W. Norton & Co.

Parkes, Graham (2003) 'Winds, waters and earth energies: *Fengshui* and awareness of place', in H. Selin (ed.), *Nature Across Cultures: Views of nature and the environment in non-Western cultures.* Dordrecht: Kluwer, pp.185–209.

Passmore, John (1980 edn.) *Man's Responsibility for Nature.* London: Duckworth Publishers.

Petrarch, 'The Ascent of Mt Ventoux', in E. Cassirer, P. Kristeller and J. Randall (eds), *The Renaissance Philosophy of Man* (1948). Chicago: University of Chicago Press, pp.36–46.

Plato. *Republic*, tr. R. Waterfield (1993). Oxford: Oxford University Press.

Pollan, Michael (2004) *The Omnivore's Dilemma: A Natural History of Four Meals.* London: Bloomsbury.

Powers, Charles T. (1997) *In the Memory of the Forest.* London: Anchor.

Raffel, Douglas (1959) *In Ruhunu Jungles.* Colombo: K.V. G. de Silva.

Rousseau, Jean-Jacques, *The Reveries of a Solitary Walker*, tr. C. Butterworth (1992). Indianapolis: Hackett Publishing Company.

Schipper, Kristofer (1993 edn.) *The Taoist Body*, tr. K. Duval. Berkeley: University of California Press.

Schipper, Kristofer (2001) 'Daoist ecology: the inner transformation. A study of the precepts of the early Daoist ecclesia', in Girardot et al. (eds), *Daoism and Ecology: Ways within a cosmic landscape.* Cambridge, Massachusetts: Harvard University Press, pp.79–94.

Schopenhauer, Arthur, *The World as Will and Representation*, tr. E. Payne (1969). New York: Dover Publications.

Sharr, Adam (2006) *Heidegger's Hut.* Cambridge, Massachusetts: MIT Press.

Thoreau, Henry D., 'Walking', in Armstrong and Botzler (eds) (1993) *Environmental Ethics: Divergence and convergence.* New York: McGraw-Hill, pp.108–17.

Thoreau, Henry D. (1999 edn.) *Walden.* Oxford: Oxford University Press.

Trilling, Lionel (1972) *Sincerity and Authenticity.* Oxford: Oxford University Press.

Waal, Frans de (2001) *The Ape and the Sushi Master.* London: Penguin.

Wang, Joseph (1998) *The Chinese Garden.* Hong Kong: Oxford University Press.

White, Lynn (1967) 'The historical roots of our ecologic crisis', *Science*, 155 (10): 1203–7.

Wittgenstein, Ludwig, *Philosophical Investigations*, tr. G. Anscombe (1969). London: Macmillan.

Woolfson, Esther (2008) Corvus: A Life with Birds. London: Granta.

Yanagi, Sōetsu (1989) *The Unknown Craftsman: A Japanese insight into beauty.* Tokyo: Kodansha.

Yutang, Lin (1936) *My Country and My People.* London: Heinemann.

Zhuang, Yue and Wang, Qiheng (2009) 'The poetics of dwelling a garden: A Confucian mode of being', in A. Laffage and Y. Nussaume (eds), *Teaching Landscape with Architecture.* Paris: de la Villette, pp.352–63.

Index

Page numbers in *italics* refer to
illustrations. 'n' following a page number
refers to a note indicated on that page.

acquisitive desire 35, 83-4
action 107, 108, 110, 150
agricultural interventions 129, 132-6
alert attentiveness 78, 91, 93, 124, 131
ambience 111
analytical attitude towards the natural
    world 40, 85, 86, 87
animals 10-11, 15, 50, 100-1
    see also hunting; wildlife
anthropocentrism 15, 26, 27, 32, 62, 102
anthropomorphism 15, 42-3, 100, 134,
    135
Arnold, Matthew 14, 28
attunement to the natural world 16, 52,
    81-106, 107, 108, 110, 131, 151, 152
    affective 83, 94-8
    cognitive 81-93, 94

Bachelard, Gaston 8, 91, 92, 93
Baker, J. A. 11 n6, 125, 126
Barnes, Simon 120 n3, 142 n3
beauty 68, 101-6, 135
    and virtue 105-6, 116, 136
Bernhard, Thomas 98
bodily cultivation 56, 75, 114-17, 151
The Book of *Liezi* 32, 85, 99, 124, 126,
    127, 129, 134-5, 146
The Book of Odes (*Shijing*) 133, 150
The Book of *Zhuangzi* 25, 35, 36, 52-3,
    59, 110, 112, 113, 121, 146, 147, 148,
    150
    compilation 20
    Guo Xiang's commentary on 33-4,
        43, 75-6, 90-1

on action 107
on animals 48, 50, 99, 100, 124, 126,
    134
on anthropomorphic delusion 42-3
on beauty 103, 104, 105
on bodily cultivation 56, 105, 115-16
on craftwork 129, 131-2
on *dao* and *de* 59, 63, 64, 70-1, 73-4,
    75, 98
on death 52-3
on hunting 123
on intellectual learning 85-6
on joy and élan 97
on man's relationship to nature 18
on nature's educative role 50
on sages 79
on unity of things 65, 66, 67, 68
on wilderness 118-19
on worldly ambitions 54
yu metaphor 55-6, 90-1
Brady, Emily 102 n10
Buddhism 15, 22, 83, 93, 119, 132

Chinese landscape paintings 17-18, *19*,
    21, 23, 31, 41, 49, 76
co-dependence 65, 98-9, 113, 138-40
Coetzee, J. M. 40
companion animals 127
compassion 10, 27, 125, 150
Confucianism 20, 22, 58, 70
contentment 96-7
convergence with nature 12, 14-15,
    23-4, 26, 28, 37, 38, 39-41, 42, 47-8,
    82-3, 112, 114, 118, 139, 152
correlatives/correspondences 51, 88, 115
cosmology 32, 51, 88
craftwork 129, 131-2, 135
culture and nature 28, 138, 139-40

dao 16, 32, 37, 47, 48, 49, 51, 57, 58-68,
    121, 131, 137, 142, 144
    accounts of 58-65
    'constant' *dao* 63, 64, 77
    estrangement from 32-6, 37, 71
    harmony with 50, 51, 56
    impartiality of 54
    ineffability of 24, 59, 62, 63, 64, 79,
        86
    naturalistic construal of 59-60, 61
    nihilistic interpretation 60, 61, 64
    pairings with virtues 74
    spontaneity 47, 77
    theistic construal of 59, 61, 66
The *Daodejing* (*Tao Te Ching*) 31, 34,
    47, 69
    compilation 20
    Machiavellian strand 20, 149, 150
    on beauty 103
    on bodily cultivation 56, 75, 115
    on convergence with nature 23-4
    on *dao* 24, 37, 47, 59, 60-1, 62, 63,
        64, 75
    on farming 133
    on intellectual learning 85, 86
    on knowledge 34
    on profound *de* 72
    on self-restraint 147
    on simplicity of life 121
    on stillness 108
    on worldly desires 53-4
de 25, 69-76, 115, 131, 142
    accounts of 69-71
    betrayal of 32-6, 71
    human *de* 71-2
    profound *de* (*xuande*) 72, 74, 76, 80,
        83
Deakin, Roger 109, 110, 120
death 52-3, 116
Dillard, Annie 15 n12, 85, 86
disillusion 11, 12, 23
disinterestedness 55, 83-4, 91, 132
dualisms 26-7
    rejection of 32, 65, 66, 67, 114, 115,
        139

eco-interventions *see* environmental
    activism
ecological crisis 26-7, 145, 146, 149
educative role of nature 50-3
élan 55, 79, 97
Emerson, Ralph Waldo 104
engagement with nature 9, 13, 107-27,
    131, 139, 151
environmental activism 9, 10, 141-2,
    145, 146, 147, 148-9, 151
environmental ethics 9, 10, 142, 143-4,
    145, 146, 152
environments
    degradation of 134, 148
    engaged creatures, dependence on
        112-13, 135
ephemerality 96
estrangement from nature 11, 24, 38, 42
    Daoist account 32-6
    technological account 27, 29-31
    theological account 26-9
estrangement from the *dao* 32-6, 37, 71
experiencing the world 14, 65, 66, 67,
    68, 71, 79, 86, 92, 110, 139

factory farming 10, 133-4
Fan Kuan 17, *19*
Faustian man 130-1, 132
Five Processes (Doings) 51, 88
flexible responsiveness 83, 131-2
Fowles, John 41, 85, 86, 120
Fox, Warwick 71 n3
Fung, Yu-lan 22 n5

gardening 14, 22, 38, 40, 49, 119, 136-40
Giono, Jean 135
God 26, 59, 61, 66
Gould, Stephen Jay 145, 146
Graham, A. C. 87 n8, 121 n4
Guo Xiang 33-4, 43, 60, 64, 75-6, 84,
    90-1, 96, 104

Han Yu 114
Hanfeizi (Han Fei Tzu) 60, 63
Heidegger, Martin 29-30, 31, 33, 36,
    108, 129

Hodgson, Noel 12-13, 28, 41
Huainanzi 51, 88, 90
humility 55, 74, 116, 132, 143
hunting 109, 122-4, 125
Huxley, T. H. 28

impartiality 78, 83-5, 96, 101, 102, 143
industrial interventions 129-32, 133-4, 141
integrity of things, respect for 102, 135
intellect, Daoism's suspicion of 28, 73, 85-6, 131
interventions in nature 108, 109, 128-46, 147, 148
intrinsic value of nature 101, 146

James, Simon P. 15 n14, 42 n7, 93 n22
Jünger, Ernst 130 n5

Kirkland, Russell 144 n8
knowledge
    intellectual 28, 73, 85-6, 131
    lust after knowledge 34
    practical 34, 73-4, 89, 107-8, 131-2
Kohn, Livia 59 n2

LaChapelle, Dolores 45 n1
language 68, 85, 87
Laozi (Lao Tzu) 22, 61, 83, 107, 115, 121, 144, 150
Lawrence, D. H. 12, 120
laws of nature 46, 47
'letting-be' 36
Li Bai (Li Po) 49, 76, 108
Liezi see The Book of *Liezi*
Lopez, Barry 12 n8, 111 n6, 151 n13

Ma Lin 17, *21*
Ma Yuan 105
Mabey, Richard 9 n3, 85, 87, 142
Macfarlane, Robert 42 n5, 49, 52
Marinetti, F.T. 29
Marx, Karl 135, 136
Mencius 33, 133
Meng Haoran 96, 108
Meyer, Jeffrey 143 n5

Miller, James 139 n17
mind–body dualism 26-7, 32, 115
mind–heart (*xin*) 32, 33
mindfulness of nature 54, 81-93, 94, 96, 97, 100, 126, 143
    see also attunement to the natural world
Moeller, Hans-Georg 63 n9, 64 n10
moods, Daoist 11-12, 23-5, 128
moral life 10, 25, 141-3, 151
Morpurgo, Michael 112-13
Murdoch, Iris 42, 54, 99
music 97, 108, 116
mystery of nature 12, 23, 24, 41, 128

nature, Daoist concept of 45-57
nature writing 8, 9-11, 142
nature-as-a-whole 46, 47, 48
Neiye 35, 66, 150
Ni Zan (Ni Tsan) 105
Nietzsche, Friedrich 61, 62, 146
non-action 36, 84, 90, 107, 137
nostalgia 11, 13, 23, 24, 120, 128
Nyanaponika 156 n22

One Hundred and Eighty Precepts 144
Ortega y Gasset, José 54 n13, 122, 124
otherness of nature 41-4, 98-101

Parkes, Graham 145 n11, 147 n12
parochial concerns 146, 148, 151
partiality 43, 55, 100, 148
perspectivism 55, 61-3, 65, 68, 85, 86, 146, 148
'philosophical' Daoism 22, 58-80, 144
philosophy, roles of 14-16
Plato 52, 115
poetry 12-13, 18, 94, 96, 108
Pollan, Michael 9 n2

qi 32, 88
quietism 54, 149, 150

rambling/roaming 55, 90-1, 108
'religious' Daoism 22, 23, 48, 56, 59, 82, 115, 144

respect for the natural integrity of things 43, 45, 55, 57, 124, 143
restlessness 34, 35, 36, 39
reverie 18, 91-3, 94, 110, 124, 137
rhetoric of convergence 39, 40
rhetoric of rights 145
rhythm metaphor 116-17
Rousseau, Jean-Jacques 9, 57, 91, 92

sages 24, 25, 67, 73, 76-80, 107
    alert attentiveness 78, 83, 124
    attunement to the world 76, 77-80, 83, 152
    compassion 76, 150
    comportment 76-7, 83, 143, 152
    élan 79, 97
    ethical life 142, 143
    impartiality 54, 55, 78, 84, 101
    relationship to natural environments 78-9, 80, 93, 114, 146
    self-restraint 147
    spontaneity 77, 121
Schipper, Kristofer 115, 116, 117 n16
Schopenhauer, Arthur 87 n8
scientific account of the world 87-90
self-centredness 98, 99
self-cultivation 9, 15, 22, 25, 142, 143, 149, 150, 151
self-restraint 147, 149
simplicity 53, 121, 149
sincerity/authenticity 70
sober joy 94, 96, 97, 98, 101, 114, 135
Spengler, Oswald 130
spontaneity 37, 46, 47, 48, 55, 56, 77, 87, 90, 97, 99, 105, 107, 116, 121, 135, 137, 146, 150, 151
stewardship over nature 27, 145
stillness 51, 75, 78, 86, 107, 108
suffering in nature 15, 98, 99-100, 101
suspension of understanding consciousness 85-7

taiji (tai chi) 114, 116, 117
Taiping jing (Scripture of Great Peace) 48
Tao Qian (Tao Yuan-ming) 18, 49, 76, 93, 94, 95, 96, 114, 119

technology
    and estrangement from nature 27, 29-31, 33
    interventions 33, 48, 129-32, 147
Thoreau, Henry David 9, 12, 100, 118

un-selfing 54, 84
unity of things 65, 67-8, 70, 71, 92
urban existence 53

vermin control 40, 41, 84, 100
virtues 10, 53-7, 69, 149
    beauty and 105-6, 116, 136
    Daoist 53-7, 74, 76-80, 83

Wang Bi 36 n10, 67
Wang Keping 103 n11, 121 n5
Wang Wei 55 n14, 105, 108
Wang Xizhi 55, 108
water metaphor 48, 51, 62, 63, 75-6, 105, 108, 150
Watts, Alan 58
the Way see dao
White, Gilbert 9
wild green-men ancestors 41, 120, 121, 130-1
wilderness ideal 40, 47, 49, 50, 118-21
wildlife 8, 39, 122-7
wisdom 34, 57, 74, 75, 76
Wittgenstein, Ludwig 63, 116
Wolfson, Esther 40, 41
wood metaphor 48, 121
Wordsworth, William 9, 52, 53, 57, 83-4
wu wei 36, 37, 78, 84, 90, 101, 107, 132, 137, 146, 147, 149

Yanagi, Sōetsu 132
yearning for convergence 11, 13, 14, 23, 131
yin and yang 47, 60, 64, 88
Yuan Ye ('The Craft of Gardens') 137

Zhuangzi 20, 33, 36, 52, 54, 61, 62, 63, 66, 79, 83, 96, 108
    see also The Book of Zhuangzi
Zong Bing 17, 18